THE ANCESTORS ARE SMILING!

Kathy Lynne Marshall

The Ancestors Are Smiling!

ISBN: 978-0-9992014-0-4

Library of Congress Control Number: 2017950074

Published by Kanika African Sculptures and Books
P.O. Box 1202
Elk Grove, CA 95759-1202
www.KanikaMarshall.com/books.html

Cover design by Mary and Kanika Marshall

Printed in the United States of America

Dedicated to the memory of my formidable ancestors
who provided me with the desire and
ability to live my life as freely as I choose:

Mary Ellen Marshall
Dr. Thomas Marshall
Daisy Dooley Marshall
Austin Marshall
Pearl Williams Carter
Reba May Williams
Otho Sherman Williams
Myrtle Booker Williams
Joseph Booker
Sara Myers Booker

Table of Contents

Acknowledgements

Although my beloved mother, Mary Ellen Marshall, passed away in 2007, she is always with me in spirit. Her "*Reflections from a Mother's Heart*" diary, contains first-hand accounts of her childhood and adult life, and was an inspiration for numerous passages in this book.

I am indebted to the following family members who provided memories and corrections to many draft versions of this African American genealogy book, including: our esteemed family historian and "Designated Genealogist" Myrtle "Lavata" Williams; the "Medical Pioneer" Charles Williams and his wife Margaret and son Bob Williams; Dale Carter, Kenora Hogan, Julie Sanders Culpepper, Alaunda Gates, Carrie Marshall Malenab, and Greg Marshall. All provided plenty of memories about our ancestors and about their own lives. My sons Isaac and Matthew Anderson, and daughter-in-law Jameillah Anderson, also responded to my probings into their young lives for this book.

Many thanks also go to several people who edited portions of this book: my patient and understanding boyfriend Michael Fitzwater, author Denise Griggs (Glass Tree Books), Dr. Deborah Pittman (professor emeritus at California State University at Sacramento), genealogist Diana Ross, and author MaryLou Anderson.

Introduction

"My favorite pastime was to catch fireflies at night during the summer. I would get a glass jar, poke holes in the lid, and catch fire flies that would light up in the jar. I also enjoyed going to our park during each day. It was about a mile away and oh so safe! People simply did not bother you in any bad way. We had swings, slides, tennis court, picnic area, pond, and lots of grass. It was between my house and my grandma's house. Both of these activities I enjoyed with my brothers and sisters. We spent many hours together doing these things. I was probably out there mostly with the boys, since I was a tomboy all the way!"

- Mary Ellen Marshall, "Reflections from a Mother's Heart"

Park down the street from the Carter's House on Walnut Street, Mount Vernon, Ohio, Photographer: Kathy Marshall, 2003

An alarming thought entered my head one day last spring as I found myself starting my 60th year of life: there are only three people older than I am in my mother's family and fewer still in my father's. Soon "I" will be the Matriarch. If I don't write a book about my ancestors, who will? NOW is the time to commemorate the lives of those who have gone before me, and of those of us still living who are their proud descendants. I have a burning desire to ensure that my family is remembered in a tangible way.

This book is a collection of true stories, creatively issued from the mouths of my family members. Some of the conversations are from regular black folk born in the latter part of the 1800s and 1900s who led difficult lives in a racially-divided America. Other stories describe remarkable successes in highly regarded fields of medicine, education and engineering. Some tales dance around our family lore that we get mechanical abilities from our enslaved ironworker ancestors. Certainly, tenacity and perseverance have driven my ancestors to ensure that each new generation is better off than the last.

As you will learn from the pages in this book, my Great-Aunt Reba Williams was mentioned on *The Tonight Show with Jay Leno* and profiled in *Essence Magazine* when she was 106 years young. My great-grandmother Ella Carter worked for Representative Columbus Delano who helped convince President Lincoln to issue the Emancipation Proclamation in 1863; and that same year, my newly-freed second great-grandmother Margaret Booker, drove her five children in a horse-drawn buckboard from Virginia to freedom in Ohio. But who else knows those interesting tales? The heartwarming, uplifting stories contained in this book illustrate that all lives matter, no matter how rich or poor, uneducated or college-educated, whether from middle-America or the southern states or from golden California. These imagined dialogs are presented by each character as though she or he is talking directly to the reader. The content is based on telephone and personal visit interviews with my elders over the past four decades, letters from those who are now the ancestors, family history binders, census data, my mother's personal journal, my father's cigar boxes full of sentimental papers and items, two biographical photo-journal books about my parents compiled in 2014 and 2015, lots of family photographs, and other pertinent documents.

My goal is to provide memorable histories in an authentic narrative form that can be passed down not only to the people in my family, but to anyone interested in learning about a resilient family, interwoven with the larger events of the day. I hope these personal revelations will resonate with, and inspire you to tell your own family stories. Never give up, the ancestors are calling for their tales to be told.

People Profiled in *The Ancestors are Smiling!*

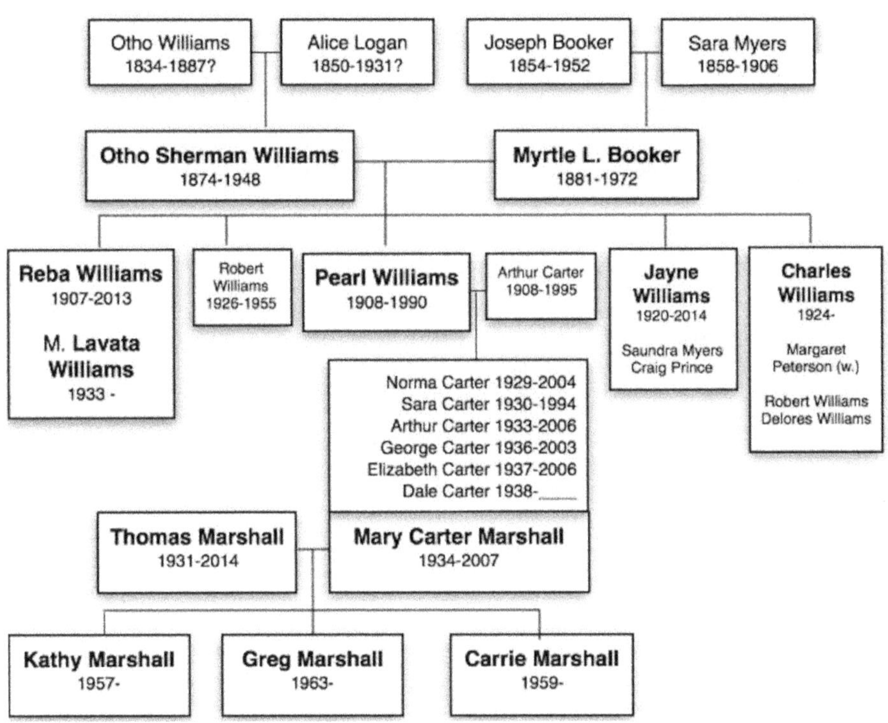

Timeline of Historical Events

*Relationship to Author Key: grandfather (gf), grandmother (gm), great-grandfather (ggf), great-grandmother (ggm)

Year	What Occurred and Where
1776	**America's Declaration of Independence from Great Britain. Slavery reigns in all 13 U.S. Colonies.**
1834	Slave Otho Williams (second ggf*) was born in 1834 in Washington County, MD.
1850	Slave Alice Logan (second ggm) was born in 1850 in MD.
1861	**Civil War 4/12/1861 to 5/9/865. The Battle of Antietam was fought in Washington County, MD, in 1862.**
1863	Emancipation Proclamation signed by Lincoln. Slave Margaret Booker drives family to freedom in Ohio.
1865	**Slavery abolished throughout America.**
1867	Otho Williams (second ggf) and Alice Logan (second ggm) marry in Washington County, MD.
1874	Otho Sherman Williams (ggf) was born 6/19/1874 in Wash. County, MD; died 1948 in Mt Vernon, OH.
1881	Myrtle Booker Was (ggm) was born 3/13/1881 in Barnesville, OH, and died 1972 in Mount Vernon, OH.
1892	Austin Henry Marshall (gf) was born 9/19/1892 in Columbus, GA, and died 1967 in Columbus, GA.
1892	**through 1964: Jim Crow Laws sanctioned segregation of blacks and whites in many parts of USA.**
1902	Daisy Rae Dooley Marshall (gm) was born 1/16/1902 in Macon, MS, and died 1986 in Cleveland, OH.
1905	Otho Sherman Williams (ggf) and Myrtle Booker (ggm) marry 1905 in Philadelphia, PA.
1907	Reba Williams (great aunt) was born 1/23/1907 in Philadelphia, PA, and died 2014 in Columbus, OH.
1908	Pearl Lavata Williams (gm) was born 10/7/1908 in Germantown, PA, and died 1990 in Columbus, OH. Arthur Taft Carter (gf) born 5/2/1908 in Mount Vernon, OH, and died 1995 in Pittsburgh, PA.
1914	**World War I begins 7/28/1914 and ends 11/11/1918.**
1924	Charles Elmer Williams was born 7/14/1924 in Mount Vernon, OH.
1931	Thomas Marshall was born 5/2/1931 in Cleveland, OH, and died 2014 in Carmichael, CA.
1933	Myrtle "Lavata" Williams was born 11/27/1933 in Mount Vernon, OH.
1934	Mary Marshall was born 4/1/1934 in Mount Vernon, OH, and died 2007 in Sacramento, CA.
1939	**World War II begins 9/1/1939 and ends 9/2/1945.**
1943	Charles Elmer Williams becomes a Machinist Mate in the Navy.
1946	Charles Williams was one of the first to survive tuberculosis from streptomycin treatments in 1946.
1957	Kathy Marshall was born 1957 in Cleveland, OH.
1958	Dr. Thomas Marshall graduates from medical school and begins military obligation as a Navy Lieutenant.
1959	Carrie Marshall born 1959 in Seattle, WA.
1963	Greg Marshall born 1963 in French Camp, CA.
1964	**The Civil Rights Act was passed 7/2/1964, finally ending segregation in America.**
1966	Mary Carter Marshall family takes train from Sacramento to Ohio to visit Carter and Marshall family.
1983	Mary Marshall (mother) is the Principal when Apple Computers donates a number of 64K Apple IIe desktop computers to her Camellia Basic Elementary School, the first Computer Lab in Sacramento, CA.
1983	First Williams/Myers/Jenkins/Walker family reunion held at Mohican State Park, Mansfield Ohio.
1985	Isaac Charles Anderson (son) born 1985 in Sacramento, CA.
1990	Matthew Thomas Anderson (son) born 1990 in Sacramento, CA.
2003	**Iraq War begins and Isaac Anderson (son) joins the Marines after high school.**
2008	Jazmine LynAnn (2008), Isaiah Christian (2010), Jeremiah Liam (2016) Anderson born. (grandchildren)
2013	Reba Williams received high school diploma at 106 years of age.
2015	Matthew Anderson (son) is the National Taekwondo Freestyle Champion in 2015-2016.

Chapter 1: The Clock is Ticking

Four Generations: Mary Marshall, Kathy Marshall, Isaac Anderson, Pearl Williams Carter, Sacramento, California, Photographer: Ken Anderson, 1986

The clock is ticking away faster and faster now that I am in my 60th year of life and longevity issues have begun creeping into my thoughts. I have been futzing around with gathering African American family history information since the mid-1970s, even before Alex Haley's *Roots: The Saga of an American Family.*[1] I have created several three-ring binders filled with printed census and other official documents for each of my six main family lines: the Williams, Marshalls, Carters, Bookers, Myers, and Dooleys. But what will happen to all of those containers full of priceless genealogy information when I am gone? Nobody can really ferret out what all those documents mean, unless they are written in a narrative form that pulls all those disparate facts together into an interesting story.

For example, it is true that my Aunt Lavata was almost kidnapped in Istanbul, Turkey, after a visit to the Holy Land! It is truer still that my father was a real Iron Man who grew up in a funeral home. It is also true that my Grandmother Daisy was allegedly the first certified African American Mortician, before she became a nurse. But who, besides my immediate living family, will ever know those things?

After my birthday in 2016, I began researching how to write interesting histories about my ancestors, utilizing as much data from official sources as possible. Initially, I had two main goals in mind. First, was to find out about my enslaved second great-grandfather Otho Williams, who was born in 1834 in Washington County, Maryland. This goal would include utilizing traditional family history research, as well as DNA testing technology to find out about our ethnic heritage. Equally as important, though, was my second goal of commemorating the lives of my ancestors who descended from the slave Otho Williams. I initially decided to dedicate myself entirely to creating one book that would explore both of those lofty goals. No more diddling around with online Scrabble games until I had completed this monumental task!

On October 1, 2016, I listened to an online webinar[2] from the Genealogist's Writing Room, an organization which encourages African Americans to start writing our own stories, instead of letting others write our history for us. They, and other sources from genealogy conferences and books, stressed the importance of starting to write a book by revealing what we already know about our own family. That means writing about myself first, then I would write stories about my parents, grandparents, and so forth. Even though I may never find out answers to all of my questions, I need to just start writing now. Those genealogy sources indicated it would be acceptable to simply acknowledge that some unknowns might have to be researched at a future date. "Start writing now" has become my mantra!

I finally understood how to begin this monumental project and I feel a strong assurance that I *will* be successful this time! The ancestors want their stories to be told and they want me to complete this inspirational writing journey *now*. Once I understood that, the words began to flow from my excited brain through my fingertips and onto my laptop computer. I am finding it easy to create an outline for the book, including about 50 questions about my enslaved ancestor, such as: Who was Otho Williams? Where did he live? Who were his parents and his slave owner? What daily duties did he perform? Did he fight in the Civil War? Was he successful after slavery? Was he a metalworker like many of his descendants after slavery? So many questions had to be researched and answered, hopefully, definitively.

Early into this process, I wrote an initial Introduction stating what I intended to do. I had read that it can be effective to write the book as we are making discoveries so the reader can share in our exciting finds, and disappointments, as the research progresses. It is motivating to know your book is actually being written! That is the tactic I am taking for this project.

The first month, I wrote feverishly about my immediate family's upbringing. I am fortunate enough to have my mother, Mary Ellen Marshall's, personal journal entitled "*Reflections from a Mother's Heart*" That means I can share heart-warming details about her childhood in Ohio, her marriage to my father, her job as a teacher and principal in California, and her thriving watercolor art business during her retirement years. This wealth of information which came directly from her memories, allows me to write her story using her own words, in her own voice.

I also have a few letters from my grandmothers and uncles from 40 years ago, containing some important family history information. Since 2006, I have been inputting official census and other documents into my ancestry.com online family tree, including relatives as far back as the end of slavery. So I have a lot of data to help write these nonfiction memoirs and accounts.

By the end of the second month of non-stop composing, I have nearly 90 pages of narratives and photographs and charts! I sent a copy of that first draft to Myrtle "Lavata" Williams (technically, she is my first cousin, once-removed, but I call her Aunt). Aunt Lavata is not only the great-granddaughter of the slave I am investigating, but also our beloved family historian. Aunt Lavata sent me back pages of typed feedback, corrections, and additional stories. Her first-hand accounts of living with my great-grandparents Otho Sherman Williams and Myrtle Booker Williams, as well as her mother, Reba Williams, were invaluable for the "16 People Lived in My House" and "A Super Star at 106!" as well as "The Designated Genealogist" chapters in this book. All of these references and resources have been carefully incorporated to develop stories that seem to come directly from the mouths of my formidable ancestors. As I write every page, I can hear them talking to me saying "No, write it this way," or "Yes, that's exactly how it was!"

In the beginning of my fourth month of work, I found several momentous "Smoking Guns" which led to exciting answers to terribly important questions about Otho Williams' parents and his slaveowners. My book was filling out quite nicely by the end of the sixth month. I even spent the first two weeks of the seventh month in Maryland doing "boots on the ground" research to see where my family lived, to smell the air they breathed, to touch the ground they walked on in the 1700s and 1800s, and to take plenty of photographs for inclusion in the book. It was truly a magical experience!

But I started having concerns that the slave research portion of the book was fairly academic with lots of charts and graphs, and the DNA chapter was somewhat technical. Both of those more scholarly segments contrasted a bit awkwardly with the folksy stories of my Williams descendants. I agreed with some of my editors that it seemed like I had two separate books: one about the slave Otho Williams and one about his descendants. So in the eighth month on this project I decided to split my writings apart into two separate books.

This book contains stories about the courageous spirits of our Williams slave descendants, as well as profiles about me and my immediate family, including my father. Many of these stories are about regular black people who lead typical, difficult, hardscrabble lives as domestics and cooks and laundresses in racially-divided America. Some stories tell of remarkable successes of their children who made their way into the highly regarded professions of medicine, engineering, computers and education. This is highly significant because it was illegal to teach slaves to read, so many black people in America have been behind the 8-ball for many generations. However, the tenacity and fortitude of my relatives drove them to ensure that each new generation was better off than the last. The stories contained in this book are not only meant for my relatives, but for anyone interested in learning about a resilient American family.

Now let me introduce you to the heroes and heroines in this book:

- My first great-grandfather Otho Sherman Williams' Ohio home was a sanctuary for up to 16 of his descendants. He was the son of the slave, Otho Williams, who is profiled in *Finding Otho: The Search for Our Williams Ancestors*, being written by this author.

- My great-aunt Reba Williams was a cook for a Pulitzer Prize winning author and who, at the age of 106, was profiled on *The Tonight Show with Jay Leno* and in *Essence Magazine*.

- My grandmother Pearl Williams Carter was a domestic employee who aptly raised seven contributing American citizens.

- My great-uncle Charles Williams survived tuberculosis trial testing in 1946 and was a Machinist Mate in the Navy.

- My aunt Lavata Williams was a Designated Genealogist, appointed by the elders as the keeper of our family history.

- My mother Mary Ellen Marshall went from a small-town existence to become a beloved educator and professional artist.

- My father Dr. Thomas R. Marshall grew up in a funeral home, but later delivered 1,000+ babies while having a great time participating in high-level sports competitions all around the world.

- Me, Kathy Marshall, my siblings, children, and grandchildren are the proud descendants of these remarkable ancestors.

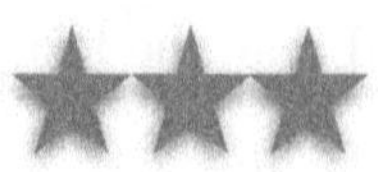

Chapter 2: 16 People Lived in My House

Otho Sherman Williams Speaks to His Teenaged Granddaughters, Mary Carter and Lavata Williams, During His Last Summer, in 1947

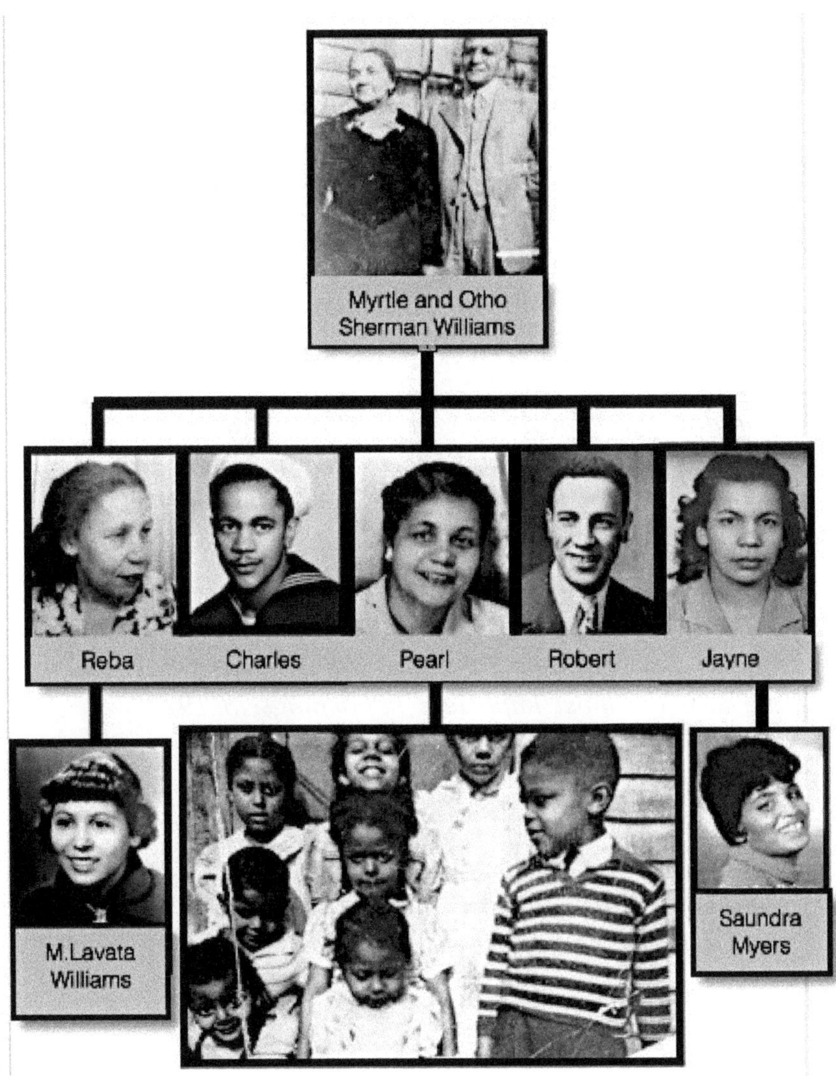

Top: Myrtle "Lavata" Williams, Sara Carter, Norma Carter
Mid: George Carter, Mary Carter, Arthur "Sonny" Carter
Bottom: Dale Carter, Elizabeth "Betty" Carter

The most momentous worldwide event that happened in 1947 was the signing of the World War II peace treaty.

However, the most incredible event that happened to Black America in 1947 was Jackie Robinson becoming the first African-American to play major league baseball, signing to the Brooklyn Dodgers! Other notable events were historian John Hope Franklin's "From Slavery to Freedom" becoming the most popular African-American history textbook ever. Further, William Dawson became the first black man to head a United States Congressional Committee, and Percival Prattis became the first black reporter in the United States Congressional press gallery.

But to the Williams family in Mount Vernon, Ohio, perhaps the most important happenings in 1947 were the family histories the Patriarch of the family, Otho "Sherman" Williams, told to his granddaughters, Mary Ellen Carter and M. Lavata Williams. It became their job to keep their grandfather entertained by playing card games during their summer vacation, as he battled dementia during his last year on Earth.

From the Mouth of Otho Sherman Williams:

How did it come to pass that three generations of family lived in my house off and on during the 1930s and 1940s in Mount Vernon, Ohio? Well, it actually started with me, the man of this large family, Otho Sherman Williams. I carry my father's proud name of Otho Williams, however, my friends call me Sherman, my kids call me daddy, and the youngest ones call me granddad.

Otho "Sherman" Williams' teenage granddaughters Mary Carter and Lavata Williams Mount Vernon, Ohio, 1947

Yes, for quite a while, there were 16 people - three generations - living in my rambling, two-story clapboarded house. I rent this house from the Cooper-Bessemer Corporation, in Mount Vernon, Ohio. We are actually living on their property in what is called a row house, at 217 North Norton Street. Believe it or not, we live right next door to the industrial engine manufacturing facility where I worked for nearly three decades since World War I!

My lovely granddaughters, Mary Carter and Lavata Williams, are spending time with me all summer long. I plan to teach them to play various card games, as well as a thing or two about my very interesting life.

* The First Day with Granddad *

Mary and Lavata, you girls have been given the enviable task of being my companions during your summer school break. It is still 1947, isn't it? Both girls nod their heads yes. Can you believe those doctors are claiming that I am losing my sensibilities? Just because I keep getting dressed every morning to go to work, even after they "retired me" at my job at the Cooper-Bessemer engine plant? Imagine that, after working there almost 30 years, they cast me out and tell me to stay home? They didn't even give me a pension after I worked six days a week. They always felt free to come and get me at night too when they needed my help! Well, I bet they will be calling me as soon as Bessie, the largest compressor on the factory floor, breaks down again. You know I am the only one who knows how to fix that old gal!

Well, as you will soon find out this summer, I love to play cards, especially for money. And let me assure you, I never lose either! My nickname has been "Foxy" all my life, but I won't tell you whether it was for my personality, or my love of card games, or for handling the ladies! (wink) All you girls need to know it that you will never be able to beat me, even though those crazy doctors say my mind is slipping away. Mary, I can tell that you are competitive like me, aren't you? Mary smiles shyly as her granddad continues speaking. You have a certain gleam in your eye, even though you are as quiet as a mouse. I bet you will turn out to be real good card player when you grow up.

> *[Author's Note: Mary became a Silver Life Master bridge player[3] during her lifetime and like her granddad, never let anyone beat her at cards, or Scrabble, or marbles, or golf, or tennis, or anything else!]*

Yes indeed, I am going to teach you two girls a thing or two during this mid-Ohio summer, and I bet you will never forget me!

"Granddad, did you really make this beautiful wall?" asked Lavata innocently as she pointed to a photograph of her granddad; he was standing next to a carefully built wall that he had made at Mr. Stillwell's house. This type of skilled construction work was how he fed his large family during the Great Depression, after his long-time employer, Cooper-Bessemer Corporation, had laid off many workers during the late 1930s. Sherman did occasional odd building jobs for Mr. Stillwell in the 1940s too. Forgetting he was now retired, though, Sherman would often get dressed in the morning and walk to his former employer's house, which required Mr. Stillwell to drive him back home. That is precisely why the granddaughters were tasked with keeping their granddad at home this summer.

Otho Sherman Williams built this wall, Mount Vernon, Ohio, c. 1945

This first morning in June 1947 with his granddaughters, Sherman had momentarily forgotten about this most recent employer. He now harkened back to his days working next door at the Cooper-Bessemer plant, where he often repaired their big compressors. His short-term memory loss is due to what we now know as dementia, or perhaps even Alzheimer's Disease. These maladies are a long term and often gradual decrease in the ability to think and remember, which is great enough to affect a person's daily functioning. Occasionally, Sherman's memories slipped back to an earlier time in his life. Physically, Sherman looked hardy and healthy, but sometimes he had a hard time remembering certain words and names of things and people.

Even with those difficulties, though, this summer his granddaughters would soon learn more than they ever dreamed about their granddad and how he grew to be the Patriarch of the family.

Mary and Lavata were 13 and 14 years old, respectively, and spent every moment they could together in their grandparent's house, along with 14 other relatives who lived there during part of the 1930s and 1940s. During the school year, Lavata lived at Malabar Farm with her mother, Reba Williams, the cook for Pulitzer Prize winning author and conservationist, Louis Bromfield. An hour or two away from Mount Vernon, Ohio, Lavata could only visit her favorite cousins during the summers and some holidays.

This first morning with their grandfather was spent outdoors on the porch, situated in three metal chairs under the shade of two large peach trees, that were laden with ripening fruit. This two-story white sanctuary house, which often housed 16 family members, was actually a row house, owned by the Cooper-Bessemer Corporation. The original house had a large porch which spanned the width of the house (note: in this photograph, their house was physically moved to another street after Sherman's death in

Williams' house, Mount Vernon, Ohio, 2009 Moved from its original location on Norton Street near Walnut Street, minus the porch.

1948). There was a two-seater swing at the south end of the porch and lots of chairs on the other end. The many children living there could play on the porch during rainy days, instead of being cooped up in the house. Mary and Lavata entertained their granddad on the porch most of the day, generally playing cards and listening to his memories all day long. There were two big peach trees in the front yard and a grape arbor, vegetable garden, chicken coop, and large-leafed maple and oak trees in the large backyard.

This first day of watching their granddad, the girls' grandmother, Myrtle Booker Williams, brought them all glasses of cool sweet tea as her husband of 42 years began to speak.

So you want to know about my life as a child, do you? Well, I was born on June 19, 1874, near the small town of Boonsboro, in western Maryland. As you know, that means I just turned 73 last week while you were still in school. Boonsboro was a town founded in 1792 by William Boone, the cousin of that fur cap-wearing fellow, Daniel Boone. The main town is located at the foot of South Mountain, between Hagerstown - the Washington County seat - and Harper's Ferry. That's where John Brown planned a slave uprising in 1859. We lived only a few miles away from the Civil War Battle of Antietam, where over 20,000 people died in one single day in 1862! I imagine you have already learned about the Civil War in school, right?

The girls look at each other quizzically, not really knowing how to answer their grandfather's question; thankfully, he keeps talking, sparing them from telling him they don't know much, nor care to know much, about any war.

I imagine my father was right in the middle of all that fighting, but I don't think he was able to actually serve in the military, though, because he was still a slave. Although, I did hear that many free-colored and former slaves fought in the Civil War after President

Lincoln issued the Emancipation Proclamation in 1863, I think it was. Since Maryland was loyal to the Union of the United States, not a what-they-called Confederate, or rebel state, their slaves were not freed until 1864. Can you imagine former slaves being able to use guns on white people who looked like their former slave owners?

The girls shrug their shoulders, because neither had ever thought about being a slave, a slavemaster, nor even what it would be like to fight in a war. They were generally more interested in going to the movies, giggling, skating, or picking and selling dandelion greens to the neighbors for a bit of pocket change. However, they listened respectfully to their grandfather as he continued to speak with a far off look in his eyes.

I just don't know whether my family participated in any way to win that war for our freedom. Did they drive a horse cart with food for the soldiers, or did they only farm wheat and corn on their master's property? Maybe they were workers inside the master's house, or maybe they went to war with their master as a personal manservant? I wonder if they had colored friends who fought for our freedom? I just don't know.

My ears hurt just thinking about how noisy it must have been for everyone who lived near the battlefields, with the constant rifle fire and thunderous cannonballs booming for days on end. In September 1862, I believe it was, the smell of gunfire and death, and seeing so many injured and dying men lying everywhere must have been horrific. It had to be terrible for the Union and Confederate soldiers, and unimaginably difficult for the local people who had to feed, clothe, care for, and bury those men.

I don't know about you girls, but I am ready to do something else besides talk all day long. Let's play some cards on the back porch. You play poker, don't you? The girls wrinkled their eyebrows and vigorously shook their heads no, being good church-going girls. After a moment, their granddad suggested something simple like the card game "Old Maid." Mary went inside, to her family's designated side of the house, to get a well-worn card deck of 52 regular cards and one joker card. Essentially, this was a simple card game, like "concentration" where players take turns matching up pairs of cards (like two kings) and discarding them on the table. The person left with only the joker card is the old maid and loses the game. Sherman and the girls played this card game until the afternoon. Then granddad said he wanted to take a little nap.

And that is how Mary and Lavata spent their first day starting to learn about their granddad, Otho Sherman Williams.

* The Next Day *

After breakfast, Sherman, Lavata and Mary met at the shaded porch swing, located on the wide porch spanning the front of the house. Without any small talk, Sherman immediately launched into the past.

Did you know, Mary, that your other grandmother, Ella Carter, used to work for Congressman Columbus Delano's family right here in Mount Vernon? The girls shook their heads no, as they often would when asked a question about their family history. Christopher Columbus Delano was a lawyer elected to several political jobs, including representing Ohio in the Congress. In about 1860, I think, he helped nominate Abraham Lincoln to the Presidency. He held several offices for Lincoln and he was the United States Secretary of the Interior for the next President, Ulysses S. Grant.

The most important thing Delano did, in my opinion, was to encourage President Lincoln to issue the Emancipation Proclamation in 1863. Well, my daddy told me a little bit about how terrible slavery was. Those white people in the states down south tried to separate from the United States, unless they could keep their slaves to do all of their work forever. Those southerners were called rebels, or Confederates. Well, once Lincoln issued that Emancipation Proclamation, colored people that used to be slaves, as well as colored people who were already free, could use a gun, and fight hard against those rebels.

My point in telling you all that was really to let know how important and powerful a man Columbus Delano was and that your Grammie Carter worked for him and his family. Imagine how many politicians she saw at the Delano house while she worked there.

We all know that Ella Carter has such a nice house, with beautiful rich folks furniture and fancy lamps and such. I think her house is paid off too! None of us really ever knew the true story of why she has been treated so well all these years, but maybe the wealthy Congressman was thankful for the special care she gave his disabled son every day. She worked for many years as his son's nursemaid. The Delano family brought Ella, age 4, and her guardians, Albert and Alice Roy, with them from Virginia to Mount Vernon in 1866. Albert and Alice were servants in the Delano home and Ella grew up with the white Delano children.

Not to tell tales, but there are rumors that the Delano family may actually be Ella's blood relatives! I do not know the name of Ella's mother or father, but some say her mother might have been from the Roy family and that she may have died in childbirth while she was working for the Delano family in Virginia. Some people think Ella's father might be one of the Delano boys, but I do not know that for sure. Maybe one day when you girls are visiting your Grammie Carter, or your cousin Kenora who lives next door to Ella, you can find out if they know the truth. All I know is that Ella Carter is much revered and respected in this town.

It would be something, Mary, if your family is somehow related to the Delano family, wouldn't it? "Yes indeed, granddad!" exclaimed Mary, clapping her hands with excitement. Sherman continued: I wonder if they are also related to President Franklin Delano Roosevelt? Hmmm, Mary you might want to look into that too.

The girls look at each other with amazement at this interesting revelation about their revered and beloved Grammie Carter. Mary tentatively says "All I know, granddad, is that my mother always forbids us from visiting Grammie Carter, and I just don't know why. Me and my brothers and sisters love visiting Grammie Carter, partly because we get to see how rich people live. Mostly, though, it is because Grammie always seems glad to see us!" Lavata chimes in "Yes, Mary's grandmother always treats me like one of the grandkids too. She asks me to come inside with the rest of her grandkids and feeds us cookies sometimes. She is always nice to all of us."

Mary hastily adds that her brothers and sisters would never break their mother's rule, for fear of receiving a whipping by a peach-tree switch. No, they would never stop by Grammie Carter's house on the way back home from playing in the park, just because her house is on the way home. Never. Both girls smiled angelically.

"I always think of Grammie Carter as a little Dutch lady because she is so fair-skinned and often wears her hair braided on top of her head, like I imagine Dutch women wear theirs. My cousin, Kenora, who lives next door to Grammie Carter, is so lucky! Her family gets to eat a big chicken dinner every Sunday at Grammie Carter's house, in that amazing dining room with the fine china and silverware" said Mary dreamily. Sherman is amused at the realization of where the kids probably "do" stop on their way home from the park. He thinks this is a good place to stop for the day, so they can get in a game of cards before his afternoon nap time.

* The Next Day *

After a hearty breakfast of eggs and bacon and freshly squeezed orange juice prepared by his wife Myrtle, Sherman energetically makes his way outside. The girls are already waiting for him, ready for additional juicy tidbits about their family.

When I was born in 1874, my father was 40 years old and my mother, who was named Alice Logan Williams, was 23. They had nine children altogether, but only seven survived past the age of five. That is just like your family, Mary. Your mother and father also had seven surviving children, right? Mary nodded her head in agreement.

My father and his older brothers Samuel, Henry and Hezekiah, and their younger sister, Margaret Elizabeth, were all slaves. There were several other slaves on the property too, most of them relatives, I think, but I don't know for sure. They all lived on a big, 200-some-odd acre property called Meadows Green, next to the Beaver Creek in Washington County, Maryland. I think they also sometimes lived in a town called Funkstown.

As you can imagine, my mother and father did not like to talk very much about slavery days. In fact, I don't remember them ever telling me their slave master's name! My father did sometimes talk a little bit about his dad, of course, but I cannot remember his name right now either. I think it was some kind of royal-sounding name though, like King or Prince or Duke, something like that.

My dad said his father knew a lot about ironworking and could fix just about anything made with metal, probably because he worked at the Antietam Iron Works for a number of years. I don't know if you heard about this from your mothers, girls, but many of us believe we Williams get our mechanical abilities from our enslaved ancestors. Just look at every generation: there are people who work with metal and can repair machines, like me and your other grandfather, Joseph Booker, here at Cooper-Bessemer. Many of us can figure out solutions to all kinds of problems.

Some of us colored folks at Cooper-Bessemer should have been engineers because of the work we do there, but because we are Negroes, we cannot join the union or be called engineers or receive anywhere near the same pay as whites.

Why, I added a laundry room with a sink and running water onto this old house so your grandmother could make a living taking in laundry from the white folks around here. Maybe it is true that my mechanical and fix-it abilities came from my ancestors, and maybe I have passed them down to you too! That is something to think about, isn't it? The girls politely said "Yes, granddad," in unison.

Starting to get uncomfortably warm outside in the front yard, the three of them went inside to the parlor. White lace curtains covered the tall, narrow, windows, muting the sunlight and darkening the room a bit, giving the perception of it being cooler inside. There was a small round table where they could lay out the playing cards.

It was the house rule that Mary's large family of eight had to stay on one side of the house and yard, mainly because they were so noisy and there were so many of them. The other seven or eight family members sharing this house had larger accommodations on the other side of the house from Mary's family. Myrtle and Sherman each had separate bedrooms upstairs. Sons Charles and Robert shared an upstairs bedroom and, for a short while, daughter Jayne had her own room. Lavata and her mother Reba shared a bed downstairs.

As was their usual follow up to a few of Sherman's interesting life stories, they played cards for the rest of the day, until Sherman started dozing. Then the girls were free to follow their own exploits.

* The Next Day *

Today, because it was raining outside, the girls sat gingerly on the good, plastic-covered, upholstered sofa in the parlor, that was mainly used for company. Their granddad sat in his comfortable easy chair, well-worn from years of repose after working six days a week at Cooper-Bessemer, or performing hard physical labor for Mr. Stillwell. Sherman resumed his life story after a few pleasantries with the girls.

My father said he and his parents and older brothers lived in a log cabin, and other slaves lived in other barrack-like cabins on the property. He said his grandmother, for a time, was responsible for all the cooking on the farm, both for the master and his dozen or so slaves. I am not sure if those other slaves were related to us or not, but I think some of them may have been. Maybe you girls will be able to find out when you grow up. The girls raised their eyebrows at that.

A log cabin similar to the one Sherman's grandparents may have lived in during the 1830s and 1840s, near Boonsboro, Maryland.

After slavery, my father and his brother, Hezekiah, bought some property in Funkstown. That is actually the place where I was born. This part of the story gets a little cloudy, though, because I was so young back then. In about 1869, my dad bought five acres of land on the road that leads to Roxbury Mills, which was next to the Antietam Creek, also in Washington County, Maryland. He built a little house on the property and dug a well. That's where we moved to after I was born, and we lived there until daddy died in about 1887 or 1888.

Part of 5-acre property near Roxbury Mills bought in 1869 by formerly enslaved Otho and Alice Williams, Photographer: Kathy Marshall, 2017

I remember all too well that it was very hard work farming that much land with hand plows and a mule, especially during harvest time. We mainly grew corn and wheat on that land, and had a pen with some pigs, and a hen house like most of our white neighbors. Mama had a vegetable garden out back so she could pick fresh fruit and vegetables for our daily meals. She was able to sell any extra food at the market (but usually she just canned any surplus harvests for the winter). We did not have grocery stores where you could just pick up and buy whatever you wanted and have it delivered to your home, as we have here in Mount Vernon. Most of us had to grow our own food and butcher our own meat.

We kids were sometimes able to walk to the colored school nearby, so we could learn to read and cipher our numbers, but I really only had the chance to go through third grade before I had to start helping out on the farm. Mom and dad placed a lot of importance on us getting an education. They wanted to be sure nobody took advantage of us, as others had done to them, simply because they could not read or write. You know that it was illegal for anyone to teach a slave how to read, don't you? The girls, wide-eyed, shook their heads no, they did not know that. Most white people did not want to be arrested, so most of us could not ever learn to read or write, whether we wanted to or not.

Well, daddy died unexpectedly when he was only 53 years old; then everything fell apart! Mama and us kids just couldn't keep up to pay the mortgage or the taxes. After daddy passed away, the Sheriff was coming to kick us out! My bossy older brothers, Edgar and Sam, convinced my mother that we should leave the land our father had worked so hard to keep. They believed we should move about 20 miles north to Greencastle, Pennsylvania. I think Edgar had some friends up there that promised to help us restart our lives in a new state. It was a long time ago, so I don't remember all the details about our escape. But one morning, just after dawn, in the summer of 1888, my momma, brothers Edgar and Sam, and my sisters Alice Virginia, Mary Irene, the baby Bessie, and I made ready to flee our home. We quietly packed ourselves and some of our belongings into a couple of horse-drawn carts driven by my dad's older brother, Henry, and my brother Edgar. We made our way carefully onto the rutted roadway, and went north to Greencastle. It took us all day on the road and we had to sleep under the moonlight that first night, but we finally made it to our new home.

I was about your age at the time this all was happening. I don't remember everything about our time in the new town, but I do know that all of us had to try to make money for the family somehow. We did odd jobs here and there just to eat and to pay rent for our little room on Jefferson Street in area where Negroes lived.

Lavata, looking very interested in how they escaped, asked "What did you and your family do next, granddad?"

As you both already know, I taught myself how to play the mandolin, an old clarinet, and the violin and banjo when I was young. If I ever needed to earn some extra money, I could always hire myself out to play with my musician friends for various events, like parades and parties, just as I sometimes do now. My family also did a little farming as laborers, drove a horse cart for people, and cleaned houses. It was all hard work. That's all I remember right now, but we survived as a family - that's the important thing.

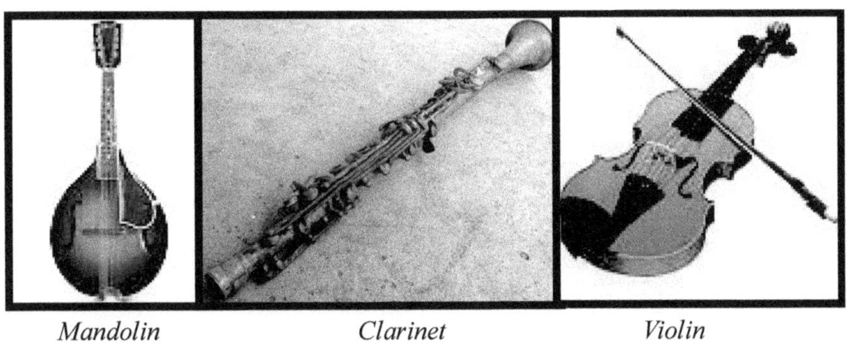

Mandolin *Clarinet* *Violin*

Well girls, I think that is enough talking for today. Perhaps we can play a little gin rummy for an hour or so, then I will need to rest my eyes for the remainder of the afternoon. The girls dutifully got up, retrieved the playing cards from the cupboard and sat down with their grandfather at the dining table to "get schooled" on how to win at gin rummy. An hour or so later, after losing every game to their grandfather, they said their goodbyes to both grandparents.

They walked quietly to the kitchenette on the other side of the house where Mary's family was allowed to live. The girls made peanut butter and jelly sandwiches - with extra grape jelly made by Mary's mother, Pearl. Finally, the cousins were able to skip happily outside to play with Mary's brothers and sisters for the rest of the day.

* The Next Day *

Good morning girls! I am so glad you came back to see me. The girls smiled a bit at the realization that their granddad did not remember they all lived in the same house and they see him every day. It should still be a little cool today with these overcast skies periodically covering up the sun, but at least it is not raining like yesterday. So what do you want to do with your old granddad today? Would you like to play some more gin rummy?

"No Grandpa. Yesterday you said you would tell us how you all survived after your family left Maryland for Greencastle, Pennsylvania," Lavata reminded him.

Both girls actually looked a little more interested today in finding out more about Sherman's life. They sat down on the porch swing again, looking at the two peach trees laden with fruit ready for picking. The bees sang their steady buzzing song around the flowers and plump fruit, as Sherman continued his story.

Oh yes. Thank you for reminding me Lavata. Last night, I remembered something else that you might find interesting. I once heard that in 1888, two of America's first banks owned by colored people opened their doors - a Savings Bank in Richmond, Virginia, and Capital Savings Bank of Washington, D.C. I wonder if they could have helped us save our land when daddy died, if mama knew about them. Oh well, that's just water under the bridge now, isn't it?

Anyway, that first few years after my daddy died were tough for all of us. As I was saying yesterday, we had to find any work in Greencastle. There were only about 1,000 colored people living there in Franklin County in the 1890s, but there wasn't much work for us. By 1900, four of our family's children were still living there. My mother was 49, Edgar was 30, Sam was 27, Mary Irene was 19, and Alice Virginia was 17. I am not sure where my sister Bessie was. But I was no longer there.

You see, I had left my family when I was about 15, off to make my own life! My brother Sam had challenged me one too many times and I was tired of him bossing me around. I, "Foxy," was smarter than all of them! Some buddies of mine wanted to see what kind of work we could find up north, so in the 1890s we headed northwest to Pittsburgh, Pennsylvania. It was a big city, at least bigger than Boonsboro, Maryland, and bigger than Greencastle! We had heard that after the Civil War, Pittsburgh became an industrial powerhouse because it had good access to water, iron ore and coking coal for making steel. There were many immigrants coming into the state from Scotland, Ireland, Poland, and Italy before the turn of the century and they claimed many of the available skilled jobs, especially in the steel industry. Rich men got richer by investing in blast furnaces and rolling mills, all to make steel manufacturing more profitable. We thought we would easily be able to get a job in a steel mill, but the Machinist's Union restricted membership to whites only, so even seasoned colored workers could not become apprentices or get union cards.

There were only about 500 colored people in Pittsburgh out of almost 80,000, if I recall correctly. Thankfully, there were many different jobs that we were allowed to do back then, such as: being day laborers, servants and butlers, hotel waiters, barbers and hairdressers, furnace workers, domestics, stablemen, hotel cooks, bootblacks, farm workers, porters, laundresses, dressmakers, bricklayers, plasterers, railroad depot janitors, messengers, coachmen, stone masons, and even firemen and cigar makers. Colored people who did some of those jobs were considered to be "professionals." Mary and Lavata looked impressed at the long list of jobs that colored people could do in a big city like Pittsburgh.

My friends and I tried to get good jobs at the American Iron and Steel Company as a "heater" but we could only get low-level jobs there like threading nuts and janitor work. When the white unions were striking, colored people could sometimes get jobs in the steel plants as strike-breakers, working at the jobs that striking workers usually did.

Girls, you may not know this, but some slaves became quite skilled in the iron forges making metal products, so the steel-making companies did hire us colored people, but they would not, and still don't, let us join their unions. That usually means we cannot earn as much as white people and we cannot get a pension to take care of us in our old age. That is what has happened to me here in Mount Vernon. We almost have to beg for help from friends and family now that they retired me. Me - the guy who knew how to fix every machine in that place! It still makes me so mad!

Back in the 1890s, my friends and I did odd jobs here and there while we were in Pittsburgh, sometimes playing music for various events, and earning a few pennies here and there. We had lots of fun as free 20-year-old boys! The girls were not sure what he meant. All they knew was that Granddad Sherman was feeling mighty happy at that moment and suggested they start playing some cards, because he was feeling lucky! He started to teach them how to play Black Jack, which ended up becoming one of Mary's favorite card games.

* The Next Day *

Sitting in the metal chairs on the porch with a biscuit and some gravy leftover from breakfast, Sherman greeted his granddaughters and asked them to refresh his memory on where he left off the day before. Oh, we were talking about Pittsburgh? Let's see, we stayed maybe a couple of years in Pittsburgh doing grunt work in the steel mills and whatever other odd jobs we could get. We heard there was more work in East Liverpool, Ohio, about 40 miles away, so we went. I quickly got a job there working as a coachman in the Lee household, which was in one of the big houses on 5th Street near Peach Avenue. Yes, Peach Avenue - that's why we planted these peach trees when we moved here!

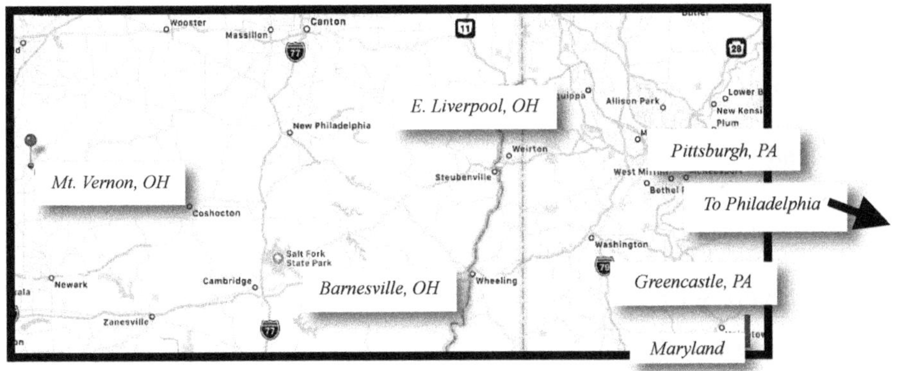

Map of Sherman Williams' trek from Maryland to Pittsburg, PA (c. 1890), to East Liverpool, OH (1900), to Philadelphia, PA (1905), to Mt. Vernon, OH (1910).

The Lee's house was located a few blocks from the Ohio River, which separated Ohio from West Virginia. It was my job to drive a horse-drawn carriage to transport the Lee family wherever they wanted to go. Sometimes I took them to visit friends, or go to work at their pottery, or I would transport various items from one place to the next. I wore a large heavy cloak and tall top hat, so I wouldn't get soaked in case it rained while I was waiting for the Lees to finish their business.

Joseph Lee manufactured pottery as part of the "Taylor, Lee and Smith" company until 1901, when he left the company. Pottery was one of the biggest industries in East Liverpool in 1900. In fact, East Liverpool was the "Pottery Capital of the USA" during the 19th and 20th centuries, because it produced nearly half of all the country's ceramic products. East Liverpool also got the name "Crockery City" because it boasted dozens and dozens of potteries by the 1880s. The city produced nearly half of all American restaurant and hotel plates and cups; they called it china. There is even a Museum of Ceramics History there. They have many examples of the types of pottery East Liverpool produced. I have seen their factory numerous times, of course, because I often had to carry heavy boxes full of pottery that needed delivering. It was a huge operation, with huge brick kiln ovens and warehouses for making, painting, and storing pottery. They made fancy ceramic teapots, mainly, but also vases and cups.

[Author's note: 100 years later, Sherman's great-granddaughter, Kathy "Kanika" Marshall, became a clay and steel sculptor.]

Here's another interesting story about the Lee household: I worked there with a cute 17-year-old servant girl named Pearl Brown, who came from Dayton, Ohio. Mary, I named your mother Pearl after that little gal in East Liverpool - but don't tell your grandmother that! Mary smiled knowingly, because her stern grandmother Williams was nobody to fool around with; it might make her angry to know how Granddad selected the name Pearl.

Now Mary, I know that your mother, Pearl, had dreams of becoming a secretary and she even went to Mount Vernon Business College for a few months after she graduated from high school in 1926. But those white folks were not going to let her be anything except a servant, maid, or cook, and I was not going to allow any of my children to sit around the house moping. So Mary, your mother had to go to work. Pearl Brown's family helped your mother get a job in Dayton, Ohio. Unfortunately, that's where she got hooked up with your good-for-nothing jail-bird father, Arthur Carter. That's a sad story that I don't want to talk about right now. I'm sure your mother has probably told you all about that anyway.

"Well Granddad, to tell you the truth, I really only remember meeting my father once when I was five and he gave me a nickel," said Mary, looking a bit forlorn. "My mother gets very angry every time someone brings up daddy's name, so we usually don't mention him."

Well then, back to my story about how I met my wife. Your grandmother was born in 1881, in Barnesville, which is the north-easternmost part of Ohio, in Belmont County, close to Pennsylvania. Myrtle's father, Joseph Booker, was an ex-slave from Virginia. In 1880, Joseph was a 24-year-old porter for a hotel, and her mother, Sara Myers Booker, was a 22-year-old housekeeper and mother of their three-year-old daughter, Maude. Joseph and Sara were light-skinned mulattos in a mixed neighborhood of whites and coloreds in Barnesville. "Mulatto" generally means they look like they had white and black blood.

The Mabras were next door to your Booker family, and the Jacksons and Fowlers were one block over on South Street. Sara's kin, John and Corintha Myers, were on Chestnut Street, and John and Cornelia Booker Myers were on Reeds Row. Your great-grandmother Margaret Booker, and her kids, lived on Vine Street. There were a few more colored families, but altogether coloreds made up a tiny percent of the population in Barnesville. We coloreds make up only about one percent of the 10,000 people in Mount Vernon now.

Mary, you look a little sleepy. You did pretty well at Black Jack yesterday. Do you want to try it again right now? Mary's eye's popped open quickly. She was a little embarrassed at having been caught dozing; she nodded her head yes. The three of them played Black Jack the rest of the day, enjoying the breeze through the maple and oak trees, and watching the birds flit here and there amongst the heavy branches.

* The Next Day *

Both girls greet their granddad when he comes out of the house after breakfast. They are already sitting in the porch swing, chatting together quietly, guessing what stories they will learn today.

Did I ever tell you the frightening story of bravery of how your great-grandmother Margaret Booker came to be in Ohio with her kids in the first place? “No, Granddad,” the girls responded brightly. You see, Margaret and all of her children were born slaves in Virginia. Your grandfather Joseph Booker was born into slavery in 1854. He was farmed out to work for another slave master and could not live with his family. Lavata, you know all about this, being an only child. Mary, can you imagine not being able to live with your brothers and sisters, or your mother, at the age you are now? You are a teenager, right?

“Yes Granddad, I just turned 13 two months ago,” said Mary. “I have the opposite problem to Lavata, though … I have too many brothers and sisters around me all the time!” she said, smiling wryly. Lavata and Sherman laughed at that.

Soon after the signing of the Emancipation Proclamation in 1863, Joseph’s mother Margaret and four of her children, climbed onto a buckboard. That is an open, four-wheeled, horse-drawn carriage with a seat that is attached to a plank stretching between the front and rear. The buckboard and horse were given to them by their former master, whose name sounded something like Early, and who was living in tiny Beverly, Virginia. Nowadays, I think it is West Virginia. Anyway, Margaret drove by the plantation where her 9-year-old son, Joseph, had been working, and quickly picked him.

The six newly freed slaves joyously left former slave state Virginia, for the slavery-free state of Ohio. What an adventure that must have been for all of them! I'm assuming they were traveling with other former slaves who were also making their way to the Promised Land. Newly freed slaves often heard the *promise* that they would receive 40 acres and a mule, because they felt they had a right to some of the land they had worked so long, for free, as slaves. Sadly, most owners did not uphold that promise, so many slaves left their former plantations and traveled to Ohio, and other northern and western states, to start their lives as free men and women.

Your merry band of Booker relatives traveled days and slept nights under the buckboard. Crossing into Ohio at Martin's Ferry, they settled in Barnesville, Ohio, about 30 miles further away from the Virginia border. There, Margaret made a living as a washwoman in her home on Vine Street. It is hard to imagine that she had enough gumption to make such an escape with her children, with all the Civil War fighting that must have been going on all around her in 1863! Maybe other slaves making the same escape had protected Margaret and her young family, as they all happily fled to freedom.

Your great Grandpa Joseph Booker and his wife, Sara Myers Booker, moved to Mount Vernon from Barnesville, Ohio, when his daughter Myrtle was about six months old, in 1881. Sara, died in 1906. Myrtle would later become your grandmother, thanks to me! By 1920, when Joseph was 64, he married Viola Symons, a

Joseph Booker (1854-1952 and Sara Myers Booker (1858-1906)

20-years younger nurse.

We were told that Joseph's father was the slave master and that the slave master's sister secretly taught Joseph to read at an early age. When he arrived in Mount Vernon, Joseph came across as being very knowledgeable, as well as very serious, so he was able to quickly get a job at the Cooper-Bessemer machinery manufacturing plant. I think I already told you that the Cooper-Bessemer brand of industrial engines and compressors were manufactured in Mount Vernon, and that it was this city's first major industry. The girls smiled politely and nodded.

All of a sudden, Sherman looked a bit confused. I am sorry girls, but I must take a break. I am not used to doing this much talking these days. Sometimes it is very hard for me to try to find the right words to speak. Go in a get me some more tea and ask your grandmother to give me some of that peach pie she made yesterday.

After the girls fulfilled his request, they all reconvened in the back yard garden where they could sit at a small wooden table and look onto the grape arbor, imagining the sweet taste of biting into a freshly-picked red-purplish grape. The girls could sometimes glimpse a squirrel bounding up the shady maple tree and they laughed at its antics.

Sherman interrupted their reverie. How about we play about an hour of hearts on the porch before our nap? After a quick game of cards, the girls find it harder and harder to leave their granddad now that they are learning so much about him … and because they fully suspect his end is near.

* The Next Day *

Before Sherman even comes out of the house to look for his granddaughters, they are already sitting patiently on the porch swing, eager to be conspirators once again to hear the secrets of their elder.

They are starting to feel that they are his chosen ones, more than their other cousins who have never heard these adventurous tales. Yes, their 1947-style Scheherazade was just like the story-telling woman from "*1001 Arabian Nights*," but his stories were all true!

Good morning girls. Do you have any questions regarding what we talked about yesterday? Did we leave off talking about your Grandpa Joseph working at the steel plant? Do you want to hear more about that?

"Of course we do, Granddad!" both girls said with maybe a little too much enthusiasm to be believable.

Ok, here is a little history about the factory next door. During the 1840's, the C.G. Cooper company built farming-oriented carding machines that disentangled, cleaned and intermixed wool or cotton fibers. They also made power machinery, plows and metal hollowware vessels. They also supplied war machinery for the government during the War with Mexico. By the 1850s, Cooper was building blast furnace blowing engines, like those used at the ironworking plants, as well as in a few early railroad steam locomotives. When I was born in 1874, their product line was steam engines, sawmills, and general machinery. They had about 200 employees at that time. I heard tell that Cooper soon entered into the world of steam-operated farm engines for a few years. Then they started expanding their production to the new Corliss engine instead, which was sold to large mills and manufacturing plants. During the early 1900's, Cooper began producing natural gas internal combustion engines.

While I was working there, Cooper merged with the Bessemer Gas Engine Company in 1929 to become the famous Cooper-Bessemer Corporation. Initially, they had me just doing grunt work, as a common laborer, like oiling and lubing the gears and other parts, and sweeping the floors, etc. By 1930, I received training as a machinist draper in the foundry, fabricating parts so that when a machine part broke down, I could make a perfect metal piece that would replace it. That is where some of that mechanical ability from my ancestors comes into play, as well as being very accurate and safe when cutting metal parts. My father told me a story about his dad, who cut off part of his thumb while working at the Antietam Iron Works, sometime before the War of 1812. I wish I knew more about him and how he lived.

By 1940, I had moved up to a mill-write position, operating vertical milling machine tools to manufacture valves and other types of equipment. Because I only had a third-grade education, and because I was colored, I could never go any higher in the organization. While white workers in unionized iron and steel manufacturing jobs made an average of $1,700 per year in 1929[4] when I started, you better believe that colored workers made a lot less, doing similar or the same jobs!

"That does not seem fair to me, Granddad, but I guess you couldn't do anything about it back then." Mary chimed in.

Changing the subject to something more interesting to Mary, she asked "So how did you and Grandmother Williams meet?"

Your grandmother graduated from Mount Vernon High School in 1899. Her father insisted that all his children had to finish four years of high school, even if they were 25 years old! The girls chuckled. You can laugh if you want to, but your great-grandfather Joseph learned about the advantages of an education, when his slave master's sister taught him to read and write. I only had a third-grade education and I got along okay in life, because I am clever like a fox and I get along well with people. However, Joseph Booker was more respected at the plant, and he certainly made more money than I did, partly because of his education, I think!

By the turn of the century, Sara Myers Booker was 42 and taking care of their daughters Maude (22), Myrtle (19), Ada (16), and

Myrtle Williams at Mount Vernon High School Year Book, 1899

son Herbert (11). The children could all read, write and speak English well and the three youngest children were still at school. Obviously, as these photographs show *[next page]*, their family was pretty well off by the turn of the century. Your great-grandfather Joseph was 45, performing the duties of a machinist at Cooper-Bessemer, but because he was colored, he did not receive the title, nor the union wages, of an actual machinist. Joseph played his cards right, though, and paid off the house they lived in, which was located far away from the noisy company housing that many workers, like us, had to endure.

America's participation in World War I slowed C.G. Cooper's shift from steam to gas, as our armed forces needed hasty production of large caliber shells. Soon, they put up a big fence around the plant, and set up a munitions department. They were producing a thousand three-inch shells a day! As a machinist, your grandpa Booker would likely have been required to fabricate various machine parts to keep that equipment running. The girls had to keep from yawning with all of this technical talk.

Sherman could sense the girls were a little bored and he suggested playing cards, letting them choose the game this time. They

Joseph and Sara Myers Booker's Children, Mount Vernon, Ohio, c. 1900

chose to get out the "Old Maid" playing cards since that was an easy game to play, and they might actually beat him, for once.

* The Next Day *

I know you are probably wondering by now how such a "Foxy" card playing, good-looking, minimally educated musician like me would meet the beautiful Miss Myrtle Lavata Booker.

“Yes, granddad, that’s exactly what we want to know about!” both girls said, perking up now.

Well, it was pure luck and a lot of hard work on my part! You see, the Booker girls had a reputation of being prim and proper, good church-going girls. Your grandmother was really a looker when she was younger and, well, I knew I just had to be with her.

We actually met in East Liverpool, Ohio, when she and her sister, Ada, were working there in private homes as domestic servants. I was still a coachman for the Lee family and just happened to see her one day. Maybe she was coming out of the church as I was passing by; I don’t remember exactly, but I told her how lovely she looked in that smart blue dress and matching hat. I found out where she worked and I kept coming around, being as charming, polite, and foxy as I knew how to be! Occasionally, I even went to her African Methodist Episcopal (A.M.E.) church to impress her. She finally came under my spell and after courting your grandmother for about a year, she agreed to be my wife. Myrtle and I were married a few days before Christmas, on December 21, 1905, in Philadelphia, Pennsylvania. Some of my sisters and brothers were living there at the time and they helped us get started on our new life as man and wife.

In about 1910, I felt a little more mentally settled after being married for five years, but I still liked to have fun and play my music in a little band, usually on Saturday nights. Myrtle and I were renting a home on Priscilla Street in Germantown, which was generally a very nice suburb of Philadelphia. However, our two-story stone house was located in the low-rent section where mostly colored folks lived. There were bars, churches, and barbershops in our five-block area.

Our home was near Potter’s Field, a cemetery of poor folks buried without headstones. I was a 35-year-old gardener working outdoors and Myrtle was 29. We had three young children by then:

REGISTRATION CARD

SERIAL NUMBER 1226 ORDER NUMBER A-2090

1 Otho Sherman Williams

2 PERMANENT HOME ADDRESS: 615 E Chestnut Mt Vernon Knox Ohio

Age in Years 3 44 Date of Birth 4 June 19 1874

RACE

White	Negro	Oriental	Indian Citizen	Indian Noncitizen
5	6 X	7	8	9

U. S. CITIZEN Native Born	Naturalized	Citizen by Father's Naturalization Before Registrant's Majority	ALIEN Declarant	Non-declarant
10 X	11	12	13	14

15 If not a citizen of the U. S., of what nation are you a citizen or subject?

PRESENT OCCUPATION 16 Molder

EMPLOYER'S NAME 17 C. G. Cooper Co.

18 PLACE OF EMPLOYMENT OR BUSINESS: Mt Vernon Knox Ohio

World War I Registration Card for Otho Sherman Williams, Mount Vernon, Ohio, September 12, 1918

NEAREST RELATIVE Name 19 Myrtle Lavatta Williams

Address 20 615 E Chestnut Mt Vernon Knox Ohio

I AFFIRM THAT I HAVE VERIFIED ABOVE ANSWERS AND THAT THEY ARE TRUE

P. M. G. O. Form No. 1 (Red) Otho Sherman Williams (OVER)

World War I Registration Card for Otho Sherman Williams, September 12, 1918

Reba was only three, Pearl was one, and my first-born son, Howard, died soon after birth. We also had a daughter named Helen who died in 1910 and my namesake, Otho Sherman Williams Junior, who also died before 1910. Colored folks really did not have access or money to pay for doctors back then, so many colored children died young.

"How did you end up in Mount Vernon, granddad?" Mary wanted to know.

Myrtle's sister, Ada, met and married the handsome George Keyes in 1904. They met in East Liverpool where he was born and raised, and where I think I mentioned she was working for a time. They moved back to Ada's hometown of Mount Vernon, Ohio, where they were renting a house on West Gambier Street in 1910. By 1915, her husband had opened his own barbershop on East Chestnut Street.

Then in about 1913, there was a devastating storm which furiously slammed into the Great Lakes area, including Philadelphia, and it destroyed many homes. We decided to move our family to Mount Vernon, Ohio, at that time, to be closer to Myrtle's family. Big thanks go to your grandpa Joseph, for he helped me get a job with at C.G. Coopers, and a house to live in on North Sandusky Street.

But World War I was coming faster than anyone wanted to believe. Even though the war actually started in 1914, it wasn't until 1917 that the United States declared war on Germany. I registered for the war effort in September 1918. The official military papers described me as a "Negro of medium height and build with black eyes and black hair." Yes, I used to have wavy, lustrous black hair, but us Williams men seem to lose most of our hair once we turn 40! Thankfully, I did not have to fight in the war.

Sherman hesitated a moment. Several long minutes went by. Let me stop here. I must be honest with you girls. My family did not move to Mount Vernon solely because I had to register for the War… but I think I will save that story for tomorrow.

"Aw come on, Granddad, don't leave us in suspense again!" Mary cajoled, but she could see my eyes were already closed, as I pretended to be asleep.

* The Next Day *

Hello girls. Did you sleep well last night? The girls nodded yes, as usual. Let's start the day this time by teaching you the fine points of playing one of your grandmother's favorite card games: bridge. It is much more complicated than hearts or gin rummy, but it is a similar concept. Go get your grandmother, because we need four players. The girls do as they're told and get their grandmother, who is still in her bedroom upstairs, putting newly-ironed clothes away. They tell her their granddad wants her to come down and play a few rounds of bridge with them during the morning. If it were any other game, Myrtle would have shooed them out of the room with a curt "No, I am busy!" But she loved bridge and wanted her granddaughters to learn how to play it. The girls grab Sherman's favorite deck of cards from the bureau in the parlor, and they all assemble at the dining table to learn a new game.

OK, I will tell you the rules, as simply as I can. As you may know, bridge is played with four people sitting at a card table using a standard deck of 52 cards. We do not use the jokers. The players across from each other form partnerships, called North−South and East−West partners.

Each deal of the cards consists of three parts: 1) the auction, where the four players bid in a clockwise rotation describing the cards in their hands; 2) the play, where the side that wins the bidding auction tries to take the tricks necessary to fulfill their contract; and 3) the bid.

Bidding is the language of bridge. Its purpose is to give information about the strengths and weaknesses of each player's hand to his partner. A bid consists of a number and a suit. The suits are named spades (♠), hearts (♥), diamonds (♦), clubs (♣) or no-trump (NT) ; NT indicates none of the previous suits. The suits are assigned value, with no-trump being the highest and clubs the lowest value. For example, a one heart bid means the pair of partners intends to take six tricks plus one, or seven tricks total, with hearts as trump.

Don't worry, girls, if this doesn't make sense right now. When we start playing, it will become clearer. Mary and Lavata look relieved.

They are not understanding their granddad's instructions very well, but it is impolite for children to interrupt an adult with too many questions.

In the bidding phase, the dealer - that will be me - makes the first call - either a pass or a bid. The auction proceeds clockwise until it is ended by three successive players saying "Pass" indicating they do not have a better play to make. The final bid becomes the "contract." This means that one pair of partners, either the East-West or the North-South, has contracted to make a certain number of tricks in a particular suit or in no-trump. As I said before, a trick is six plus the number indicated in the bid. The girls are feeling more and more inadequate to learn this game.

Sherman continues: the first player to name the suit of the final contract – or the first to bid no-trump, becomes the "declarer." The person to the left of the declarer makes the opening lead play, and the declarer's partner, called the "dummy," places his hand face up on the table. At this point, the "dummy" becomes an observer while his partner, the "declarer," plays the cards from his own and from the "dummy" hand. Again, don't worry, this will become clearer as we play. I promise.

A pair of players fulfills its contract by winning tricks equal to or more than the number bid. When a pair does not make its contract – does not take the tricks required by the level of the bid – there is a penalty. Essentially, that is the game of bridge in a nutshell. Simple, eh? The girls are unconvinced and a bit afraid to begin playing this complicated game.

The four of them attempt to play bridge for a while, with Sherman paired up with Lavata, and Myrtle paired with Mary. Sherman and Myrtle work with their partners to coach them on the auction, the bid and the play. Many stumbles and starts occur as Myrtle and Sherman work with their acolytes. Time passes by more quickly than the usual day of storytelling and Mary finds she rather likes the game, although Lavata would rather be doing anything else than playing bridge!

Sherman gives up and proposes they break for a late lunch then take a nap for the rest of the day. The lunch sounds good to the girls, but they beg off napping and seek approval to go out and pick dandelions for their business instead. Sherman agrees and they part for the day. The girls carefully pick greens from the yard, place them in a large basket, and go from neighbor to neighbor, selling their freshly picked greens.

* The Next Day *

Today, there is a slight breeze and the two girls and their grandfather resume a morning of storytelling under the welcoming branches of the peach trees. Myrtle decides to join them today. She finds another chair and sits down to listen for a while.

OK girls, I tried hard to think of a good way to tell you the real reason we moved to Mount Vernon. There is no other way than to simply tell you the truth: your grandmother left me. She moved out because I wasn't acting like a responsible husband and father. Myrtle nods her head somberly, her lips pressed together tightly.

The girls looked shocked at this because their granddad Sherman always seemed to be such a responsible leader of their family.

It is true. Your grandmother took both Reba and Pearl in 1916 or 1917 from our home in Germantown, to live with her parents in Mount Vernon. You see, I wasn't called Foxy for nothing! I couldn't help it that the ladies liked me, a lot, in Philly - that's what we fun-loving types call Philadelphia. And I am sure you can see why they would swarm around me! Sherman winks mischievously at the girls, but Myrtle frowns and clears her throat menacingly. The girls look at each other and smirk, but without seeming to be too disrespectful.

So what if I liked playing card games and honky tonk music more than working at a boring job for a white boss? Well, your grandmother gave me the choice of supporting my family or going to jail! Of course, I chose to keep my freedom and move away from the exciting fast life in Philly to be with my family in the sleepy little town of Mount Vernon! The good thing is that your grandmother Williams really has been a happier person being so close to her family. It is also good that your mothers, Pearl and Reba, got to be close to their cousins for the first time in their lives. So I guess everything worked out for the best! Myrtle chimes in with "Amen and hallelujah, you know that is true! God is good!" then she goes back into the house, happy the truth of his heathen behavior in Philadelphia was finally acknowledged.

Sherman resumes his story. By 1920, I was performing general labor duties at C.G. Cooper, basically doing whatever low-level tasks needed to be done. During that stressful time when my wife was so furious with me, her sister Ada suggested that Reba and Pearl live with her for a while until Myrtle and I could settle our differences. I didn't know this at the time, but I was later told that Ada forced Pearl to do some strange walking exercises, alongside brick walls, to help straighten her bowed legs. I still cannot picture in my mind what was all about, but I do know that living with thorny Aunt Ada was not pleasant, that much I can assure you!

You have probably guessed that I am very different from the Bookers. Myrtle's father was very strict with his children so they were always serious, organized people. But me, I like to have a lot of fun, playing my music, and making people happy. Yes, your grandmother Williams and I are very different from each other. We are both

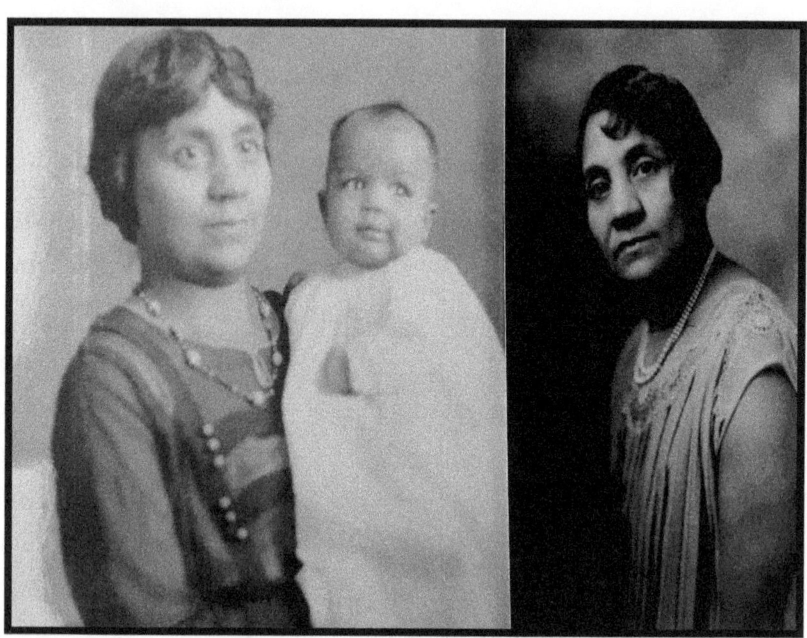

Myrtle Williams with Baby Jayne Williams in 1920 and Myrtle in the 1930s

extremely independent individuals. I do what I want in my bedroom and she does what she wants in hers.

Anyway, in 1920, Myrtle was 35, Reba was 12, Pearl was 10, and we had a brand new baby, Jayne Elizabeth. We lived on West Vine Street, the same street where your other grandmother, Ella Carter, lived on at the time. Our entire family was listed as mulatto on some government papers, as our skin color was generally like coffee with lots of milk. There were only a few other colored families on our street among the majority of white neighbors. My son, Charles Elmer, was born in 1924, and Robert "Bobby" Williams was born in 1928. Finally, some boys in this house!

The 1928 Mount Vernon City Directory correctly reported me as working at the Cooper-Bessemer factory and living on North Norton Street in a rented company home right next to the factory. While it was helpful to live next door to your workplace during the snowy weather, the factory constantly belched smoke and noise 24-hours a day. Years later, people noticed that many who lived close to the factory developed cancers and other health conditions. I wonder if that is why the doctors say I have these problems with my memory?

By 1930, I was working as a machinist at the Cooper-Bessemer foundry, repairing equipment and fabricating new parts when necessary. The house on Norton Street contained me, Myrtle, and our children Jayne, Charles and Bobby. Myrtle and I had separate bedrooms, as did Jayne. However, that all changed when Pearl had to move back home. The rent-free house she and her husband Arthur Carter had been living in was no longer available, so they, and their baby daughter Norma, moved in with us.

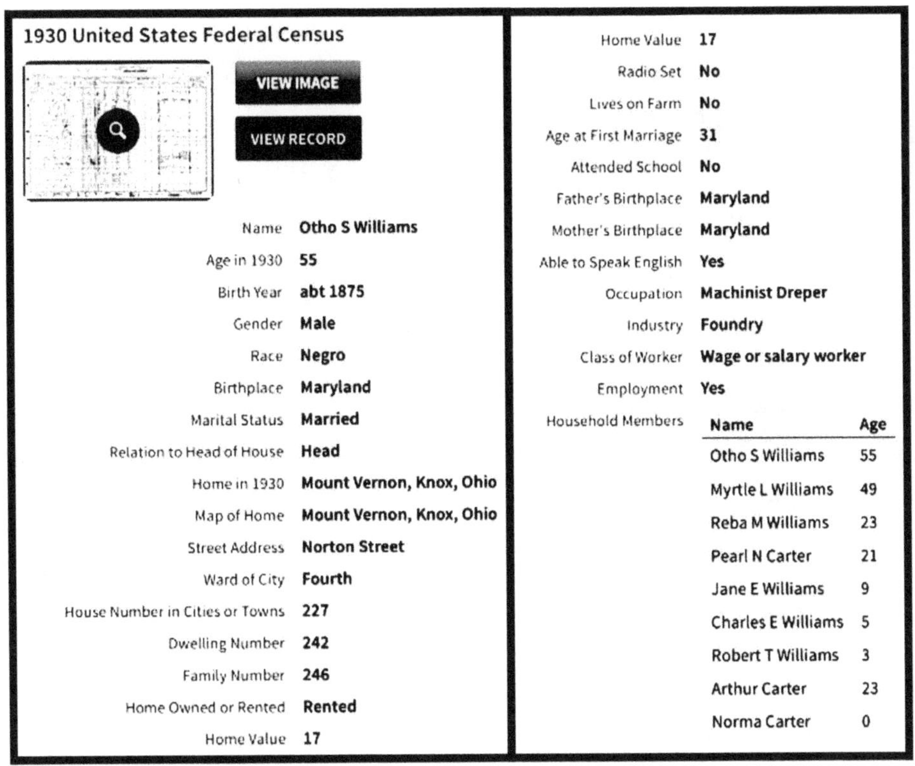

1930 United States Federal Census

VIEW IMAGE

VIEW RECORD

Name	**Otho S Williams**
Age in 1930	**55**
Birth Year	**abt 1875**
Gender	**Male**
Race	**Negro**
Birthplace	**Maryland**
Marital Status	**Married**
Relation to Head of House	**Head**
Home in 1930	**Mount Vernon, Knox, Ohio**
Map of Home	**Mount Vernon, Knox, Ohio**
Street Address	**Norton Street**
Ward of City	**Fourth**
House Number in Cities or Towns	**227**
Dwelling Number	**242**
Family Number	**246**
Home Owned or Rented	**Rented**
Home Value	**17**
Home Value	**17**
Radio Set	**No**
Lives on Farm	**No**
Age at First Marriage	**31**
Attended School	**No**
Father's Birthplace	**Maryland**
Mother's Birthplace	**Maryland**
Able to Speak English	**Yes**
Occupation	**Machinist Dreper**
Industry	**Foundry**
Class of Worker	**Wage or salary worker**
Employment	**Yes**

Household Members

Name	Age
Otho S Williams	55
Myrtle L Williams	49
Reba M Williams	23
Pearl N Carter	21
Jane E Williams	9
Charles E Williams	5
Robert T Williams	3
Arthur Carter	23
Norma Carter	0

1930 U.S. Federal Census, Mount Vernon City, Knox County, Ohio

Reba was working as a domestic and still living with us in 1928 until she got a job in Columbus, Ohio, with the Hairston family. But Reba had to move back home in 1933, pregnant, to have you, Lavata. So Jayne had to give up her long sought-after solo bedroom and began sleeping in Myrtle's room.

There was a little area off the dining room, which was only large enough to put a 3/4 size bed; that is where Reba and Lavata slept. The dining room was where the coal stove was. There was a hole in the ceiling about one foot in diameter that let a small amount of heat rise to warm the second floor bedroom area. Reba and Lavata were the warmest of all of us, being so close to the stove!

Myrtle was then about 49, and five of our children were living with us: Reba (23), Pearl (21), Jayne (9), Charles (5), and Robert (2).

For Pearl and her growing family, I had a 16'x5' kitchen added onto the house. Mary, your father was a 23-year-old car washer at a garage, but he did not usually live with us. He would reappear just long enough to make another baby. In fact, Mary, you were actually born in a house on Sandusky Street in 1934, a few blocks away from our house, because there simply wasn't enough room at my house for another baby to be born!

There were so many young children in my house under the age of 10 by the late 1930s! From Pearl and Arthur, there was Norma, Sonny, Sara, Mary, Betty, and Dale. There was also Lavata, Jayne and Jayne's daughter, Saundra, from Jayne's brief marriage to Paul Myers.

How did we feed all of those people? Of course, everybody over the age of 16 had to work, cleaning houses or babysitting, or whatever else they could find. Everyone had to bring their money home to help the entire family survive. Younger kids were sometimes left to fend for themselves after school, with Myrtle watching the preschoolers while she took in laundry and ironing from white folks. We had a garden in the yard with greens and corn which barely fed us, and we got food from the church. I had to work for Mr. Stillwell in the late 1930s, making brick walls and patios and other home renovations when Cooper-Bessemer laid off workers during the Depression.

Mary and Lavata, it is too bad that neither of you two girls had fathers while you were growing up. Lavata's father was unknown and Mary's father was put into the Ohio Penitentiary a couple of times for not supporting his family, and for other offenses like "taking a car without the owner's knowledge." Can you believe that excuse? From 1942 to about 1956, Pearl received some financial aid from the government, after she officially divorced her husband. I warned Arthur

1940 United States Federal Census

VIEW IMAGE

VIEW RECORD

Name	Sherman William
Age	65
Estimated Birth Year	abt 1875
Gender	Male
Race	Negro
Birthplace	Maryland
Marital Status	Married
Relation to Head of House	Head
Map of Home in 1940	Mount Vernon, Knox, Ohio
Street	N Norton Street
House Number	217
Farm	No
Inferred Residence in 1935	Mount Vernon, Knox, Ohio
Residence in 1935	Same House
Sheet Number	3A
Number of Household in Order of Visitation	42
Occupation	Mill-rite
House Owned or Rented	Rented
Value of Home or Monthly Rental if Rented	8
Attended School or College	No
Highest Grade Completed	Elementary school, 3rd grade
Hours Worked Week Prior to Census	70
Class of Worker	Wage or salary worker in private work
Weeks Worked in 1939	22
Income	260
Income Other Sources	No

Name	Age
Sherman William	65
Myrtle L William	59
Reba M William	33
Pearl L Carter	31
Charles T Williams	15
Robert L Williams	13
Norma D Carter	10
Sarah L Carter	9
Arthur L Carter	7
Mary E Carter	6
George W Carter	4
Elizabeth A Carter	2
Dale E Carter	1
Lavata William	6

1940 U.S. Federal Census, Mount Vernon City, Knox County, Ohio

that he was never allowed to enter the house again, nor see Pearl again, for fear he would make another mouth that he wasn't going to feed. For many years, until you were 15, Mary, it was me and your grandmother Williams who helped support so many people. It certainly takes a village to raise a child!

By 1940, I had promoted to millwrite,[5] and Myrtle was a laundress who made $312 by working every week in 1939. Also still living in the house in 1940 were Reba - working as a maid in a private home - and Pearl - doing general cleaning in a private home. Charles, Robert, Norma, Sara, Arthur, Lavata, and Mary were going to school. George, Elizabeth, and Dale stayed home with Myrtle during the day.

Pearl, Reba and Charles Williams, circa 1940s

Thank goodness, that most of the time people got along well in the Williams house. However, Mary, we had a rule that all of Pearl's family had to stay in her kitchen and the bedroom allocated to them. None of you were allowed to enter our side of the house.

Mary, I cannot imagine the close quarters that you eight people lived in, but it was the best we could do for you at the time.

"Oh my goodness, granddad," said Mary, "we did not realize all that was going on at the time. We only knew that our family was never allowed to go on your side of the house or yard. We always thought we were just being punished for some unknown reason."

> *"My mom over the years would get anxious when she found herself in tight places. Eventually I learned she shared a small closet as her sleeping quarters when growing up."*
>
> *- Julie Sanders Culpepper*

> *"When we moved to our other house with more space, the pastors at the AME church would come in from out of town because we couldn't find one that would live and stay in Mount Vernon. My grandmother Williams surely would have the minister over and what a meal she would make! (called "putting on the dog"). She did not entertain a lot, but when she did, WOW!"*
>
> *- Mary Ellen Marshall*

That was not our intent, Mary. It was the only solution we could come up with at the time. But I think we should break for today, don't you? I'll try to think up something interesting for tomorrow.

Do you want to practice bridge again? Oh, that's right. We only have three people today. Ok, let's play some Black Jack in the back yard this time. Are you girls feeling lucky? Do you think you can beat me this time? Both girls nodded vigorously.

* The Next Day *

Did you know that we have German blood? The family story is that your great-grandmother Sara Myers, had a grandfather named Philip Myers, who immigrated to Maryland from Mainz, Germany, in 1766. If the story is true, Philip's family goes way back in history to the 1600s, in a place where Jewish people usually lived. Maybe you two will be able to learn more about our German ancestors when you become adults. John and Corintha Myers live in the neighborhood. You should visit them one day and ask them more about their Myers relatives.

Now let me talk a little bit about your amazing grandmother Myrtle Williams. When she was growing up and during the first decades that we were married, before all you kids came along, your grandmother was fairly active in the African Methodist Episcopal church. Your Aunt Viola Booker (Myrtle's stepmother) would organize dinners for sale to help the church. The church ladies had a sewing club, meeting at least once or twice a month. Don't let me forget to mention that Myrtle was also an Eastern Star.[6] I believe that was due to her father's wishes, because a male in the family had to be a Mason[7] in order for a woman to be an Eastern Star, and Joseph was most certainly a skilled Mason.

Most anything socially that your grandmother got to do outside of the home was because Mr. and Mrs. Newsome would invite her to accompany them. Those social visits keep Myrtle very happy.

You can take this next fact to the bank! Your grandmother is the most organized person I know. Every night before she goes to bed, her next day is already planned in detail, with the amount of time needed to complete each task. While I was still working, she was always up by 6 AM ensuring that my breakfast was ready and my lunch bucket was packed. In the wintertime, that meant she had to remove the used ashes from the coal stove, then build a new fire in the stove, the first thing each morning.

Early Monday mornings, taking care of the laundry was next. That chore meant heating buckets of water on the cooking stove and carrying buckets of hot water to the washer in the washroom. The only running water and sink in the house was in the washroom, but that room had no heat. In the winter, the water spigot must be kept open slightly, to run constantly in order to keep the pipes from freezing and bursting.

I have never seen anyone who loves to iron like my Myrtle! She adores ironing the shirts of the local white professionals. They are pure cotton, so she washes them first, hangs them outside on the clothes lines to dry, then sprinkles them with water, rolls them up to let the water evenly spread throughout the shirt, then applies starch to the clothes before ironing them. Then a flat iron has to be heated on the old coal stove. Actually, she generally has two irons, one is heating, while she irons with the other. She hangs the ironed shirts all over the house so she can admire her work. Those professionals bring their clothes and table linens over by the laundry basketful every Monday morning.

The Carter girls in dresses customized by their mother Pearl. Betty, Sara, Mary, Norma Carter, 1940.

Myrtle also had a treadle sewing machine[8], which was used by our daughters as well as herself. When her old employers gave her their old clothes, she would rip them apart and make them into a modern garment. Mary, your mother, on the other hand, was given school clothes for her children, because it was common to give clothes to poorer families who had multiple kids. Since those clothes were all the same style, Pearl and Myrtle would embellish them, adding a bit of colorful fabric at the neckline or changing the length of the sleeves, so people would not know where the clothes came from. Reba had to buy your clothes, Lavata, because you, as an only child, did not qualify for the free-clothes program.

Reba and Pearl each bought themselves the first sewing machine that Singer sold after World War II - the Feather Weight Electric. Myrtle made many clothes without buying a pattern; she would make her own designs and patterns. I think that is another source of evidence of the machinist or engineering ability that each generation got from our enslaved ancestors: being able to make your own patterns and renovate or design your own clothes.

As you both know, my youngest daughter, Jayne Elizabeth, is a very private person. It is hard to know what she is thinking behind her beautiful wide smile. For a time, she was almost like an only child because her sisters, Reba and Pearl, were 12 and 13 years older than Jayne, who was born at the beginning of the Roaring 20s. Four years later, as I think I already mentioned, Charles was born in 1924, then Robert in 1928. Excuse me if I repeat myself sometimes.

Jayne was special to us. She was calm, very quiet, thoughtful, very proper in her speech and manner. She was also very smart, earning a place in the Science and Honor Clubs at Mount Vernon High School. She was also in the Art, Girls' Reserve, and Girls' Athletic Clubs.

JAYNE ELIZABETH WILLIAMS
College — 16
Girl Reserve (3)(4); G.A.C. (1)(2) (3)(4); Science Club (3); Art Club (3); Honor Club (1).

Jayne Williams, Mount Vernon High School Class of 1938

Yes, my Jayne was wise beyond her years except, maybe, when it came to choosing men! She married Paul Myers, your not-so-distant cousin, in 1939, I think it was. When she married, they rented a room on the second floor of Mrs. May's house, just a few houses down from us. Their daughter, Saundra Lee, was born that next year. Jayne decided to improve her work opportunities by going to Mount Vernon Business School at night.

Jayne E. Williams, Mount Vernon, Ohio, 1938

Lavata uncharacteristically interrupted her granddad by saying, "Yes, granddad, we know. Especially me. I was seven years old when Jayne decided to go to Business College and she asked me to watch her baby when she was gone at night. Grandmother Williams took me aside and told me it was my job to sit at Saundra's crib, and not to take my eyes off her. If she did something that seemed odd, I was to run down the stairs and get Mrs. Mays. Truthfully, I did not really know what 'doing something odd' meant, but I did as I was told." Her granddad responded, "Good girl! It is never wise to question Myrtle's orders!" Lavata continued with her story. "It was dark when Aunt Jane got back from school. I was very scared of running home in the dark, so I didn't take time to use the sidewalk, but instead, cut through the neighbors' yards. In the summer, I would also watch Saundra on Fridays when Grandmother Williams would do her shopping, as well as most of the days during the summer. Aunt Jane would give me a dime and I thought I was rich! I have always had a warm spot for Saundra in my heart because she took her first steps to me when she was two years old!"

Sherman smiled, then continued talking about Jayne's life. You know, her husband Paul was not at all nice to her. You are too young for me to tell you all the terrible things he did, but his behavior resulted in a quick divorce soon after Saundra was born. A couple of years after that, Jayne married the handsome Waverly Glover, right before he was sent to fight in World War II. That marriage dissolved soon after he returned from the War.

Thankfully, Jayne's decision to go to night school turned out to be a brilliant one because it enabled her to take the Civil Service test and get a Federal job at Wright-Patterson in Dayton, Ohio. I heard that before she got her first paycheck, Jayne would buy chocolate bars. She disciplined herself to only eat one square at a time when her funds were low and she could not purchase food. Jayne was determined to ensure that she could provide a better financial life for herself and daughter. She would save something from each pay check even if it was just a penny. After a year of working in Dayton, she sent for her daughter to join her in Dayton. Despite Jayne's intelligence and years of experience as a Government civilian employee, she was not paid at the same rate as her white counterparts, nor promoted as the men were.

Jayne Williams on bowling league, Dayton, Ohio, 1956-57

Jayne met her third husband, Courtland Prince, in Dayton and they married in 1946. He provided a good home for her, Saundra, and their new baby boy, named Courtland Prince Jr. In her spare time, athletic Jayne would participate on the Wright-Patterson bowling league.

Jayne always had a fascination for learning, reading, medicine, and science. She often spoke fondly of her grandfather Booker's extensive book collection in his home library. Jayne used to read as a means to broaden her life in Mount Vernon.

Well girls, I guess that is all I have to say. I have really enjoyed having your company this summer and hope you will remember me and my stories, and will pass them on to your children.

Now let's play cards!

[Author Note: Otho Sherman Williams died a few months after this last summer with his granddaughters, on January 27, 1948. This is the same month and day his granddaughter, Mary, died in California, on January 27, 2007 - 59 years apart from each other. Reportedly, when Sherman died, his body stayed in the house for three days and every day several people came by to pay their respects and to pray for him. Sherman had been a very social and likable fellow. The A.M.E. Chapel had a large following of parishioners who gave him a good "home-going" celebration.

As was the way with so many aspects of American life, since Sherman was a black man, he was not allowed into the Machinist's Union, and therefore was not given a pension when he retired, even after nearly 30 years of service to Cooper-Bessemer. It wasn't until later in 1948 that the International Association of Machinists membership opened to all, regardless of race or color.

After her husband died, it was difficult for Myrtle to pay the bills. In 1955, their beloved son "Bobby" died of appendicitis at the young age of 28. Their son Charles married Margaret Peterson, but he couldn't find steady work in Mount Vernon. Sherman's youngest daughter, Jayne, was then living in Rome, New York, with her third husband, Courtland Prince;

she told Charles there were plenty of work opportunities there. So Charles moved his new wife and his mother, Myrtle, to Rome. Myrtle moved back to Mount Vernon in the late 1960s to live the rest of her life with her daughter Reba. Myrtle passed away in Mount Vernon, Ohio, in 1972.

After retiring at the age of 55, Jayne began a career as a Librarian in Columbus, Ohio. Jayne encouraged her children and grandchildren to read American and World Classic books. This tradition was passed on to Jayne's grandchildren Alaunda, Leaunda, and Thomas Gates, and Lisa Fort. and Jayne's great-grandchildren Joelle Gates-Bassett, in California. During frequent visits, as well as during the times she lived in California, Jayne enjoyed introducing her young descendants to the joy of reading.

Daughter Pearl Williams Carter passed away on January 8, 1990. Granddaughter Mary Carter Marshall passed away in Sacramento, California, on January 27, 2007. In Columbus, Ohio, Reba passed away on August 3, 2014, followed that same year by her younger sister, Jayne, on December 26, 2014. All are buried in Mound View Cemetery, in Mount Vernon, Ohio.

The information contained in this chapter was derived from numerous and varied genealogy documents (census, military records, etc.), verbal and written accounts from Sherman and Myrtle's 93-year-old son, Charles Williams, from his 79-year-old grandson Dale Carter, and mostly from his 84-year-old granddaughter, Lavata Williams.]

The Ancestors Are Smiling!

Chapter 3: A Super Star at 106!

From the Mouth of Reba May Williams

I don't know why everybody is making such a big deal about me getting my high school diploma at 106 years of age! Jay Leno told my story one night on his TV show,[9] after the Associated Press had broadcast my story all over the news wires in America.[10] And can you believe that Essence Magazine put a picture of me, Reba Williams, in their December 2013 edition? See, I am sitting up in my bed in my white cap and gown. It was all too much hullabaloo! Just the same ol' same ol'[11] to me.

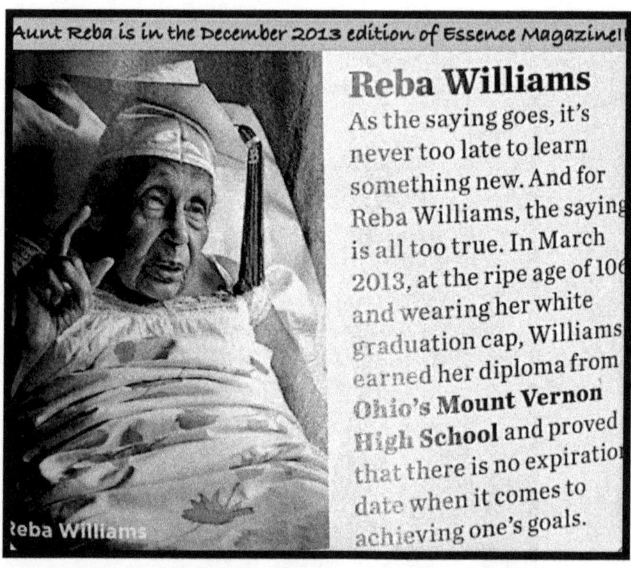

Aunt Reba is in the December 2013 edition of Essence Magazine!

Reba Williams

As the saying goes, it's never too late to learn something new. And for Reba Williams, the saying is all too true. In March 2013, at the ripe age of 10 and wearing her white graduation cap, Williams earned her diploma from **Ohio's Mount Vernon High School** and proved that there is no expiratio date when it comes to achieving one's goals.

Reba Williams profiled in Essence Magazine, December 2013.
Photo by Dave Polcyn, Associated Press.

How did this Super Star status happen to me at the tender age of 106? You may not believe it after I tell you my story, but I really have always loved reading. My Bible is always at my side, along with large-print novels and the Guideposts.[12] We get books from our Mobile Book Library at the Senior Complex where I live with my daughter, Myrtle "Lavata" Williams. My grandfather, Joseph Booker, was a slave in Virginia. Joseph learned to read and write from the sister of the plantation owner. I say all that to let you know that education has always been very important in my family, even during slavery times when it was illegal to teach slaves to read and write.

So here is my unbelievable story: Back in school, I had completed all my requirements for 12 years of high school in 1925. However, my teacher assigned us to do one final book report on a book I had already read. I refused to write the report again because I didn't like the book. They would not give me my diploma without the book report, but I wouldn't budge. The school even asked me to take it home and read it over the summer and said they would give me the diploma if I wrote a report. I said the book was not worth reading and I'd already read it once, didn't like it, and I wasn't going to read it again! So the teacher wouldn't let me graduate with the rest of my class. Now understand me, I *do* believe in education and I wanted my diploma, but I was very strong-willed (and still am!). That means I went through the next 88 years without a high school diploma, all because of a silly book report and my stubborn pride!

A retired Mount Vernon English teacher, Rita Dailey, my daughter Lavata, and some of her old school friends, went to the School Board a few months ago and asked whether they would award me with my diploma now that I am in my twilight years. One day, a newspaper reporter from the News Journal in Mansfield, Ohio, a cameraman, my younger brother Charles (only 88 years old) and his family, and my daughter, all squeezed into my bedroom here in Columbus, Ohio. Mount Vernon Superintendent Steve Short read over my high school records himself, and was on hand to personally award me with my long-awaited diploma.

I admitted to the reporters that I hope current students realize that learning is important and that they probably should not follow my stubborn example. "If they expect to get any place in this world, they have to learn," I told the Journal. I was never against school or

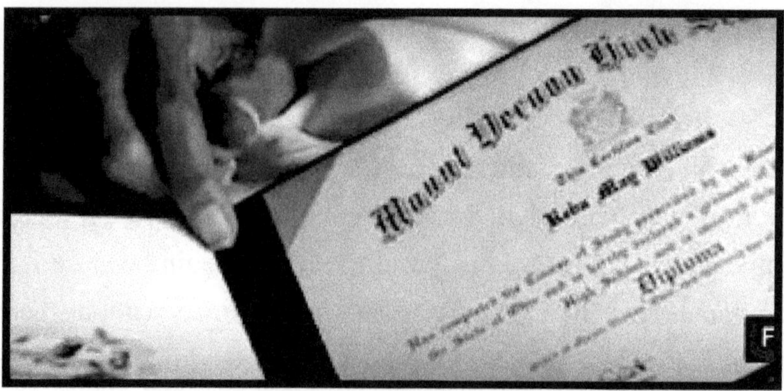

Reba Williams gets high school diploma in March 2013 at 106 years of age

learning, but on the contrary, I grew up wanting to read rather than run around and play games like hide-and-seek with the other kids. I told the reporter my favorite subject was math, but I didn't care for history.

The reporter asked me lots of questions about my life, especially working as the cook for Pulitzer Prize winning author, Louis Bromfield, at his Malabar Farm in Lucas, Ohio. I responded that my boss, Mr. B.- that's what I called him, was just regular folks. He was just the same to everybody, no matter how famous or regular they were.

I initially worked at Malabar Farm in 1943 as "the second girl" cleaning and dusting, making beds and serving dinner each night. When the cook got time off every two weeks, I was assigned to do all the cooking from Friday through Monday. I soon got a promotion, though, when the regular cook took her usual two days off and didn't return! So I was in charge of the kitchen from that point on. I felt like it was my very own place that I could organize and run however I chose. I loved the huge, industrial, cast-iron stove with two ovens. The stove was between the door to the outside and a good sized window, allowing the kitchen to get ventilation when it was needed. There was plenty of counter space and cabinets full of dishes and mixing bowls, and what-

Malabar Farm Kitchen, Photograph granted by OhioTrek.com

Malabar Farm, Lucas, Ohio

Reba Williams, cook,
Malabar Farm, Lucas, Ohio, c. 1943

not, next to the large white Frigidaire refrigerator. Yes, I enjoyed being queen of this kitchen. Mr. B. had rambunctious boxer dogs that he let tear throughout the house, except that I stared them down; those spoiled dogs didn't dare come into my kitchen!

Mr. B. had a small little house for me and my young daughter next to the big house, where his family lived. Lavata was bussed to school with other kids in that lush rural area. She was the only young person on the farm, which must have been very lonely for her. During the summer school breaks, I sent her back home to Mount Vernon, Ohio, to be around her cousins and my parents.

Working at Malabar Farm was quite an experience! Lavata and I even got to witness the marriage of Humphrey Bogart and Lauren Bacall at the farm, because Mr. B. had the event catered. He invited us to enjoy the wedding and reception. Besides Bogey and Bacall, Mr. B. welcomed several stars like Tyrone Power, James Cagney, Kay Francis, and George Burns and Gracie Allen, who all wanted to get away from the big cities to relax and enjoy nature.[13]

Mr. B. was a believer in implementing various farming techniques to conserve the land and water. In 1942, when he wrote "*A Primer of Conservation*," he had divided the land in America into fourths. He felt one fourth had already been destroyed and another fourth was already half-way to deadliness. A third fourth, because of its location, was progressing more slowly along the same path. The last fourth was largely undesirable for agriculture, but makes for beautiful scenery.

He believed there are tried and true methods to save our soil, conserve our supply of water, prevent floods, and the devastating effects of droughts. Some of these methods include reforestation, contour plowing, terracing, and strip planting. He often said:

> *"The problem of soil and water conservation is our gravest and most fundamental national problem. It is the duty of every citizen, for his own welfare, if for no other patriotic reason, to support and fight for and possibly initiate measures having to do with conservation of soil, water and forests."*
>
> *-Louis Bromfield*

This was certainly the best job of my life. I was his cook at Malabar Farm from 1943 to 1957, until he died. Then I needed to find other employment.

Being the cook for a famous man certainly wasn't my only job throughout my life. I was born on January 23, 1907, in Philadelphia, Pennsylvania. My parents were Otho Sherman Williams and Myrtle Lavata Booker. I was the oldest child, followed by Pearl, Jayne, Charles, then Robert. My family moved to Mount Vernon, Ohio, when I was only six years old and my sister Pearl was five; that is where my Booker grandparents were living.

Most of my adult life, aside from Malabar Farm, was spent working as a housekeeper doing day's work in white folks homes, mainly in Mount Vernon, Ohio. That was just about all a colored woman was allowed to do back then: clean, cook, or do laundry. Colored people generally didn't have unions or retirement plans, and we hardly made any money at all, so we had to work until we were very old. I didn't stop working until I was 82! For the next 25 or so years I have lived with my daughter in a Senior apartment complex in Columbus, Ohio. Until a few years ago, I was still able to get around pretty well using a walker. But the bones in my spine kept curving inward as I got older making it harder to stand up straight; they call it osteoporosis. Thank the Lord, I could still do a lot of personal things for myself. In fact, I would get real peeved when people tried to help me with my walker; I would swat them away. I have always been a strong person who knows what I do and don't want in life. Soon after we attended the wedding of my great nephew, Everett Sanders IV, in June 2009, when I was only 102, I fell and hurt my hip. I have been in this bed ever since. My hospital bed is set up so I can use the side rails to readjust myself whenever I want. I can pull myself closer to the rail to make it easier to eat from my food tray. I am lucky my arms are still pretty strong, so I can adjust myself in the bed, when needed.

Reba Williams with her walker, Columbus, Ohio

My daughter, Lavata, makes sure I get two meals a day, precisely like I want them prepared. I expect her to carefully measure out exactly three ounces of cooked diced turkey, two ounces of mashed carrots, green beans, applesauce, and mashed potatoes, six ounces of milk in a bottle with a lid, and three ounces of juice. Every dinner must be prepared the same way, just so.

Every Thursday, my daughter gives me a bath. After hurting my hip, my daughter cut off my long dark braid into this short hair style so it is easier to take care of. I must humbly admit that my moist milk

Reba Williams in her bed, eating the same precisely-prepared dinner every night by her daughter, Lavata Williams. Columbus, Ohio, 2012

chocolate skin is still smooth and almost wrinkle free, thanks to my African ancestry.

I like having company visit me, but people just ask too many questions! So sometimes I choose to remain silent and often keep my eyes closed. I like it when people don't know whether I am asleep or awake, so I can hear what they are saying without them knowing it! Usually, my daughter will repeat their questions loudly and clearly, then I take a moment to think before I answer. My memory is still pretty sharp, especially when it comes to experiences from the old days when I was growing up and when I was still working.

I remember one day when my grand niece, Kathy Marshall, came all the way from California to interview me about my life. She had all kinds of questions about how I grew up, who my grandparents were, what my life was like, and things like that. Then Lavata asked, "Mother, do you think it was possible that your Grandpa Otho Williams' slave master could have been his father? Kathy thinks Otho's white father's family might have married into the Royal family in England; that would mean we are from royalty too." Well, I don't remember knowing anything about my grandfather, except that he was a slave, so I really couldn't say yes or no to that story. Wouldn't it be something if it was true though? Royals who do nothing but have everything, compared to slaves who do everything but have nothing?

When I turned 100 on January 22, 2007, my church and "Around Town News in Columbus" made a wonderful DVD of my life in Mount Vernon and at Malabar Farm. They even had my voice singing in the background.[14]

You know, when I was young, my mother worked for an opera singer who gave me and my sister Pearl voice lessons. Believe it or not, there was the Woodward Opera House[15] in little Mount Vernon! My sister and I sang for many and various occasions, and I was singing "Whispering Hope" in the background on that DVD. The local TV news station did a story on me and my friends and family gave me a nice birthday party. Additionally, Columbus' Northland News was kind enough to mention me in a news article on TV.[16]

Lavata mailed my 100th birthday DVD the next day to my family in California. Kathy said she played that DVD for her mother, Mary, who was in a coma when it arrived on January 26, 2007. Kathy telephoned us afterward to tell us that she believed Mary could hear my voice singing on the DVD. Mary was told that her mother Pearl, and that dearly departed brothers and sisters were waiting for her to join them *in the beyond*. Kathy said that listening to my voice singing, "called her mother home" that very night …

In another interview in 2012 (I can't remember the interviewer's name),[17] I explained that one of the many differences nowadays, over when I grew up, is that our food used to be really fresh, because you grew it yourself in your own backyard. When you got ready to cook, all you had to do was go out and pick what you wanted for your meal. Back in those days, farms with cows and pigs were located right around your area; therefore, your meat was always fresh too. So we were lucky to grow up with good, nutritious food.

You see, my dear, when you get to be 106, you don't quite see things in the same way. Remember, when our food was left over back in the 1920s and 1930s, we didn't have the refrigeration facilities to keep it fresh for long periods. Potatoes, apples, and certain vegetables could be kept all through the winter in a cold basement. We also had fruit trees and my mother would can the fruit, so we could have delicious fruit all year round. It was an entirely different way of living than we have now with our modern conveniences.[18]

Back then, all people, including children, were expected to be busy. Each year there were certain things that children could do around thc house, like keeping the house dusted and taking care of younger siblings. For example, I was 13 years older than my sister Jayne, so I was like her second mother. At that time, not only did the father work, but the mother worked too - at least colored mothers did - so the children had to help out at home.

When the snow was high, you walked in a single file through a path cut into the snow. Of course, nowadays, you can just telephone to find out how each other is doing, but back then, we didn't have telephones and we had to walk to visit our friends and relatives.

On the whole, I must say I enjoyed my life. I worked hard and constantly, and walked every place I needed to go, before I hurt my hip. I have enjoyed every new era, adapting to the new times, not holding onto the old ways of doing things. Even though I always say it's the same ol' same ol', I really do find interest in new ideas and new ways of doing things in this world.

One last thing: Lavata and I were talking about the Christmas memories that she used to include in our Christmas letter. How many of these items can you remember from your own family?

- Christmas wreath on the door and glowing candles in the windows.

- Sears and Robucks' Christmas catalog pages ragged from wishing.

- Christmas music from the radio filled the air with anticipation.

- Lists of Santa wishes tucked in chimney's damper on the coal stove.

- Bread drying in a large enamel basin for the making of sage dressing.

- The homemade fruitcakes stored in a large tin pail months before the finishing touches.

- Stockings hung behind the old coal stove. Disobedience meant switches instead of candy and an orange or apple.

- Christmas morning when we grandchildren would creep down the cold stairs very early and very quietly in the morning to a beautifully decorated tree full of glittering lights and ornaments. Wrapped presents were placed under the tree, and unwrapped toys from Santa.

[Author's Note: Reba May Williams was born in 1907 and passed away peacefully at her home in Columbus, Ohio, on August 3, 2014, at the age of 107. Her thoughts presented in "A Super Star at 106!" were derived from the Associated Press news reports, taped Jay Leno TV segment, December 2013 Essence Magazine, a 2012 news interview, numerous documented interviews with her daughter, Lavata Williams, and nephew, Dale Carter, and from personal visits by the author in 2003, 2009, 2012, and via telephone conversations with Reba and Lavata Williams on many other occasions.]

The Ancestors Are Smiling!

Chapter 4: Day's Work Raised a Family

From the Mouth of Pearl Lavata Williams Carter

"My mother, Pearl Lavata Williams Carter, was my hero. She spent her days rearing seven children by herself. She gave her every day for our sake. It was amazing she could rear us on being a domestic employee! She cleaned houses during the day and doctors' offices at night. We always had food to eat. She cooked the same thing each day - like Thursdays were baked beans and hot dogs or Spam. It was always good tasting food. She served our plates from the pot because there was no leftover food. Mom also made sure our small housing space was clean. We did not live in a negative environment - ever! Mother always went to church each Sunday and dressed for the occasion. She wore hats, gloves, and high heels. She generally chose flowery types of of fabric for her dresses and made most of them herself. Her favorite color was blue. She crocheted well. She played Cuberson bridge, and belonged to a bridge club that she hosted once a year. After she divorced my never-present father in 1942, mom did not date, except every other year a fellow came from New York and they would sit on the couch and talk."

- Mary Ellen Marshall, "Reflections from a Mother's Heart"

Raising seven children on a domestic employee's salary? I never thought that would become my life's legacy! I wanted to be a secretary after I graduated from high school in 1926. I was not going to be like those other colored girls who got pregnant right away and had a bunch of babies and cleaned other peoples' houses all their lives. No, I was planning to go to Business College after getting my high school diploma. I would work in an office, taking dictation and typing up correspondence from the boss. I would be respected as a professional office employee. But life doesn't always turn out as our childhood dreams wish…

I guess I should begin from the beginning. I was born on October 7, 1908, in Germantown, a neighborhood inside Philadelphia, Pennsylvania. My daddy, Otho Sherman Williams, moved us to a two-story house made of brownish-gray blocks after he and my mother,

Myrtle Lavata Booker, got married in 1905. Germantown was the birthplace of the American antislavery movement, so they were pretty accepting of colored families moving in. It was also the site of a Revolutionary War battle, the location of the first bank of the United States, and the residence of many politicians, scholars, artists, and social activists of the time. Some of dad's family lived close by, but there was nobody my age and we lived there only a few years.

House opposite to where the Williams rented a house in Germantown, PA, 1905

Our Williams family moved to Mount Vernon, Ohio, in around 1916, probably to be closer to my mother's family, since that is where she was raised. My grandfather, Joseph Lewis Booker, was born a slave in Virginia in 1854. I was told that he was responsible for helping to keep the farm equipment running on Mr. Early's plantation. After the Emancipation Proclamation in 1863, his brave mother, Margaret Booker, packed up all of her formerly-enslaved children. She drove them all by horse and buckboard into Barnesville, Ohio, where she lived until 1911. After 1881, Joseph moved his wife, Sara Elizabeth Myers, and his daughters Maude and Myrtle, to Mount Vernon, Ohio. Daughter Ada was born soon thereafter, then son Herbert in 1889.

Being familiar with machinery and being able to read well made it easier for Grandpa Booker to get a job at the C. G. Cooper steel factory in town (later called Cooper-Bessemer). When my family arrived from Germantown, Grandpa Booker got my daddy a job there too, learning how to build machine parts. Daddy's 1918 Draft

Registration Card indicated that he was 44 years old, that we were living on East Chestnut Street, and that he was a molder for C. G. Cooper Company.

My earliest memory was my mother combing my thick, wavy-curly black hair to get ready for church. My older sister, Reba May, and I put on our prettiest dresses to get ready for our first photograph in 1910 when I was two and Reba was three. My mother often dressed us in pretty clothes, which she designed and sewed herself.

Reba (left), Pearl (right), 1910, Courtesy of Lavata Williams

Daddy's father, Otho Williams, was a slave in Washington County, Maryland. We were told he worked very hard after slavery and was able to buy property for his family. My daddy and both of my formerly-enslaved grandfathers always wanted more for themselves and their families. Hearing their family stories also made me want more from my life too.

In 1920, we were living on West Vine Street in Mount Vernon, Ohio. At that time, it was only me and my sister, Reba, along with my parents. We were all considered to be mulattos because of our light skin and shiny hair, but that did not mean we were treated well like white people. We could only go skating on Monday nights and to the movies on Fridays. Daddy worked away from the house everyday while Reba and I went to school, and mother took in washing once a week. The Ella Carter family lived across the street, down a block from us. They had a lot of boys, but I didn't pay them much mind, me being a shy 12-year-old girl at the time.

It was so very nice being close to my family in Mount Vernon now because we had a lot more cousins to play with. My immediate family was growing too. There was my older sister Reba, born in 1907, me in 1908, Jayne Elizabeth who came in 1920, Charles Elmer in 1924, and Robert Lewis in 1928. There was also a baby, Otho Sherman, who died right after birth, and Howard and Helen who also died young.

Otho Sherman and Myrtle Williams' Children

As a teenager, I enjoyed reading, doing puzzles, tatting, knitting, and playing bridge like my parents taught me. From my mother, I learned how to wash and iron clothes. She had a successful business doing laundry, like shirts and fine linen tablecloths and such for some of the white professionals in town. They would have their maids bring sacks of clothes and fine linens to our house on Mondays, and mother would scrub them in a little side wash room that daddy built for her, then hang them up to dry in the breeze. Ironing was mother's specialty. She had to be careful not to soil the clothes with dirty ashes from the fireplace; that's where the irons were heated, then used to press the generally white linens. The maids would pick up the clothes and linens nice and clean, and so white and stiff from the starch that mother used. Mother earned $312 doing laundry in 1940; that was something special for a colored woman at that time!

When I lived in Mount Vernon, going to school with mostly white children, I was expected to learn as much as I could. My sister and I have always loved reading: traveling to far away places and meeting interesting people within the confines of our imagination. I have been a very quiet person all of my life and would rather listen than run my mouth like fast girls did in my neighborhood.

There were only five colored students in my senior class and we were all listed on the last page in the yearbook: Eudora Davis and Howard White were in the college course, Edna Byrd and I were in the English course, and Walter Mayo was in the commercial course. Edna later married into the family.

WILLIAMS, PEARL

English course 16 credits

"She's eager to learn and thankful for good turns."

Pearl is not very talkative, but that makes her a better listener.

Mount Vernon High School Year Book, 1926

In Junior High School, I started dreaming about a life different than the typical colored woman had in Mount Vernon. Most of them had a bunch of children before they were 25 years old and were doing "day's work" in white folks houses. Day's work included house cleaning, maybe a little light cooking, janitorial work, and sometimes taking care of the children while their mothers went out to play bridge, etc. That was absolutely not going to be my life!

You see, as I mentioned earlier, I had planned to be a businesswoman. I would get my high school diploma in 1926 and enroll right away in Business College. I was going to be a secretary. I admit that was a lofty aspiration for a young colored girl in Mount Vernon in the mid-1920s, but I knew I could do it. I would make enough money to have my own pretty little house with the proverbial white picket fence out front. I would pack my suitcases and travel all around the world, visiting the places in Europe and India and China that I had only read about in books. Romance was not going to pigeon-hole my life like it did other colored girls in town. Not at all!

Well, I made it through Mount Vernon High School with decent grades. We were all told in high school that if you get a good education, you can have the world at your fingertips; but I didn't understand that really only applied to white people. I had planned to be successful, smart, and very happy, but dreams are not guarantees…

One Sunday, I was leaving the A.M.E. Church near our house where we regularly worshipped. Out of the corner of my eye, I noticed the very handsome Arthur Taft Carter looking at me with those smoldering sienna brown eyes. I smiled shyly at him, trying hard not to blush, then glanced down at the sidewalk and continued walking home. We had lived down the street from his Carter family some years ago, but had not paid him any mind then. I was raised in the church and was a good girl. I was not going to mess around with any boys before I got married. No sir! But the next time I went to church, he was there again. This time he came up to me and spoke, saying how pretty I looked with my church hat and white gloves, and how nice my short Flapper-wave hairstyle looked on me.

Pearl Williams, 1926

Arthur started coming to church every Sunday after that. He finally got up the courage to ask my daddy if he could come around to the house and visit me. My daddy didn't want to see me possibly get hurt by this smooth-talking, spoiled boy. But on the other hand, Arthur's mother was Mrs. Ella Roy Carter who lived in a beautiful house on West Vine Street. Ella was well thought of because she worked for the very important Columbus Delano family. Columbus Delano was an Ohio United States Representative and one of President Lincoln's closest advisers. He had encouraged Lincoln to issue the 1863 Emancipation Proclamation and advocated for federal protection of

Ella Roy Carter, Mount Vernon, Ohio, 1863-1962

Ella Roy Carter's Vine Street House, Mount Vernon, Ohio, 2009

civil rights for us Negroes. Ella took good care of Columbus' disabled son. I think they rewarded her with this beautiful little fairytale house, which was exactly what I dreamed about. Regardless of his mother's sterling reputation, though, my daddy did not give his approval for Arthur to court me. After all, Arthur never finished high school, rarely went to church, and was known to be a bit of a roustabout.

But all that did not matter, Arthur kept greeting me after church or whenever he saw me without my father. It did not take long for me to fall head over heels in love with that man. Every time I even thought about him, my heart beat loudly and my cheeks blushed. All my big plans about finishing Business School and becoming a secretary went out of my head every time he looked at me. I couldn't imagine my life without him.

Even so, I was able to fulfill part of my dream, and did go to Mount Vernon Business College for a few months after high school, but the people there were not very welcoming. A colored woman couldn't get a job as a secretary in Mount Vernon anyway; I would have to go to a big city like Columbus. Well, I couldn't just sit at home daydreaming about Arthur Carter. I had to work. I think it was daddy's old coworker in East Liverpool, Pearl Brown, whose family helped me get a job as a domestic working in Dayton, Ohio, about two hours away. It was absolutely the last thing I wanted to do, but here I was, doing day's work after all, just like the other colored women in town.

Secretly, Arthur would come and see me on weekends in Dayton and we would go out to the movies, get some ice cream and have a little fun. He got me to talk a little bit, but usually he was the one that did all the talking. He had grand plans for his life. He was going to be a successful businessman and he was going to have a big house and a fashionable car and make a lot of money. Yes, he sure was a talker! And he sure was a looker!

One warm summer evening in August 1928, Arthur and I left the theatre after watching a funny movie starring Charlie Chaplin, called "The Circus." Arthur reached down to kiss me goodnight, but this time it was different. He was breathing hard and his kiss was getting stronger. He suggested that we go somewhere … Months later, when I told him I was expecting a baby, Arthur asked me to marry him (I am pretty sure my daddy and his mother "encouraged" him to do so!). My parents and Arthur's mother made sure we got married as soon as possible once they found out I was expecting a child. At the last minute, we decided to elope with a brief wedding ceremony held on March 7, 1929, in Dayton, Ohio.

My new mother-in-law, Miss Ella - as I called her - let us stay with her after the marriage. Our first child, Norma Deaine Carter, was born almost three months after the wedding ceremony, on May 29, 1929. We were allowed to live with my mother-in-law almost one year as newlyweds, while Arthur's brothers, Roy and Richard, were living there too. She was none to happy about the circumstances. I could stay in her home a little while with my precious newborn baby while Arthur worked as a porter, but soon I had to get back out there and work, leaving my mother-in-law to watch my daughter during the day.

By 1930, my daddy, Sherman, was renting a two-story company row house, located at North Norton and Sandusky Street, right on the property where the Cooper-Bessemer steel factory sprawled out almost a block long and wide. It was always very loud around our house, with bells ringing and sirens blaring at all times of the day and night, generally to announce shift changes. You would think the air would always be smelly, due to the smelting of iron ore in the blast furnaces to make steel, but they must have had some kind of filtration system that seemed to reduce the industrial smells. The only time it was quiet around our house was on some holidays. Up to 16 family members lived in this house, off and on, until daddy died in 1948. That house became a kind of sanctuary for our Williams families, as more and more children - mainly mine - needed a roof over their heads during the hard economic times of the Great Depression.

My husband, Arthur, got odd jobs here and there, sometimes working in an auto repair shop because he adored cars, or he would do who knows what else during the day. He seemed to do more talking about finding work than actually working! In 1930, we were living with his mother the first half of the year, then we lived with my parents the second half (and I ended up living with my parents for the next 15 or so years!).

I had another baby in 1930, whom we named Sarah Lavata Carter; it was important to my Myers elders that we carried on the family middle name of Lavata. I also had a baby boy, Ronald, who died right after birth in October 1931. After each baby was born, I had to go back to work as soon as I was able, leaving my babies with my mother, Myrtle, to babysit.

Arthur started traveling out of town a few days a week, supposedly trying to find work. He spent more time away from Mount Vernon and his family than I was happy about. I had two living children and was pregnant with a third in 1933. This time it was a boy that we named Arthur "Sonny" Lewis Carter. By then, my husband was gone most of the time. I was fuming mad and my parents were extremely upset too. This is not the life I had planned for myself! Thank goodness my mother was able to watch the children while I had to work every day. Often, I also had to work at night doing janitorial duties for a doctor's office.

On Easter Sunday in 1934 my fourth child, Mary Ellen, was born. In 1936, George William came along, then in 1937, Elizabeth "Betty" Ann Carter came into the world, followed in 1938, by Dale

Edward Carter. I had seven stair step children that I was mostly raising by myself, with the considerable support of my parents.

Whenever my husband would come home again after "looking for work" he would apologize so sincerely for leaving us behind. Then he would hug me the way I like to be held, and brush my hair like I like it to be brushed, and tell me he loved me, etc. Each time, I would be trembling mad at him at first, but I would always let him sweet-talk me back into our bed, since I was so starved for affection. Then I would find myself pregnant once again, adding to my parents' household.

Pearl Carter (left) and her stair-step kids

The devastating Great Depression of the 1930s was difficult for everyone in America, but especially for us Negroes. My parents often ended up housing 16 family members at once, because we couldn't make enough money to have our own homes. By the late 1930s, living in this rented row house were: my daddy Sherman, my mother Myrtle, my uncle Charles, my uncle Robert, my sister Reba and her daughter Lavata, my sister Jayne and her daughter Saundra Lee, and me and my seven young children.

My family was only given one 12'x12' bedroom for all of those children, and I slept in a little kitchenette that we were able to use. It was extremely cramped. We were not allowed to go to the other side of the house where everyone else lived. My children were not allowed to even talk to their grandparents. It was very hard on all of us. Daddy was extremely angry at my husband for not taking care of his family. Truthfully, he was very disappointed in me, too, for allowing my husband to create so many babies.

After the birth of Dale, I was through with Arthur Carter for good! Daddy had also reached his limit and told my husband he was never to come to the house again, because we all knew another baby would be brought into this world; a baby that Arthur Carter would leave for someone else to feed and clothe.

I finally filed for divorce in November 1941, once I learned that Arthur was in jail in the Ohio State Penitentiary for "driving away in an automobile without the owner's consent." In the Court of Common Pleas in Knox County, I "prayed to the judge that I might be divorced from Arthur, that I be granted custody of my children, and that my children and I could have reasonable alimony and all proper relief, in accordance with the law." Thankfully, I received up to $70 per month in Aid to Dependent Families with Children until 1956, when my youngest child, Dale, turned 18 years of age. That money certainly helped me feed and clothe my family with the bare necessities of life, along with the pittance I earned as a domestic employee all those years.

I was absolutely, unequivocally, done with men! I never spoke particularly highly of the male sex after that, which may have colored my daughters' opinions of men too.

I had been deeply hurt by Arthur and was simmering with anger the rest of my life. I was now the woman I vowed never to be: raising a pile of children on a domestic employee's meager salary. I was doing housework, light cooking, washing and ironing clothes, in addition to janitorial work at night. It was hard physical labor and every night I walked home, very tired, sometimes struggling to walk, sometimes even having to lean against a tree trunk while I caught my breath. I would return home to my large family every night only to cook and clean for them too. I have no idea why I never thought to teach my children how to cook and clean more than I did. I certainly had enough of them to take that burden off me!

I was exhausted every day and my health paid the price for it. Over the years, I had developed diabetes and I had a bad heart. My limbs ached from the constant stooping and scrubbing that came with janitorial duties. But I had no pension and needed to support myself, so day's work occupied my existence until I was in my early 70s.

I did finally get an answer to my daily prayers! My large family got huge break when our A.M.E. church let me start renting an old two-story, brown shingle-clad house on Walnut Street for $7 per month. This certainly was a lot more room for all of us! There was at least one member of my Carter family living there from the late-1940s until Sonny's death in 2006!

Carter family home, 101 Walnut Street, Mount Vernon, Ohio, 1949-2006

A year or so after my father died in 1948, his rented company house was moved from Norton Street to another location, just behind my house on Walnut Street! When that happened, my mother moved in with my brother Charles and his wife to Rome, New York, for about 10 years. There, Charles was able to get a job as a Machine Shop Teacher. But from about 1959 until she passed away in 1972, my mother lived with Reba and Lavata in a house on 205 Howard Street in Mount Vernon.

My family had so much more room in this "new" (to us) two-story house on Walnut Street! I felt very fortunate to be able to rent it so affordably. Downstairs was a huge iron stove in the middle of the first floor. You had to be careful walking around the hot stove, though, to get to the stairs or the kitchen so as not to be burned. Upstairs were three bedrooms and a large bathroom with a claw-foot tub. The children had to take turns taking a bath once a week…in the same water. Admittedly, the last child was bathing in filthy water! The bedrooms were small. It was freezing cold upstairs in the winter and sweltering hot in the summer, but it was all ours! We could go wherever we wanted in that house and we could be as loud as we wanted. By the time we moved into this brown-shingle house, though, Norma was already 20, Sara was 18, Sonny was 16, Mary was 15, George was 13, Betty was 12 and Dale was 11. Most of the kids did not have the opportunity to fully enjoy the increase in space. As my children got older, they could help me more often on my cleaning jobs and we stayed afloat financially. But one by one, the children grew up, married, and moved away, until only Sonny was left in that house with me.

My health had deteriorated significantly by my late 60s. I had been an avid reader most of my life, as was my mother. One day, mother read in the Reader's Digest magazine that if you see a halo-like light around another light, you should be checked for glaucoma. The next time I went to church, I saw a halo around the church lights; the rest is history. My mother, my sisters Jayne and Reba, and niece Lavata, all developed glaucoma, but my mother and I were the only ones who became nearly 100% blind in our 70s from the conditions; the others opted for surgery.

> *"Many summers my mom [Betty], brothers and I would visit Mount Vernon for a week. My mom did not drive at the time, so my dad would drop us off on a Sunday and come back the following Sunday to pick us up. If we wanted to go anywhere, we had to WALK! We spent lots of time at the park and corner store. Our Uncle Sonny lived with Grandma Carter and he would keep a stash of Pepsi. We would come in and want one so bad, but he very seldom would let us have one. He would give us some change to spend at the corner store. One day grandma Carter was not at home. Dale and George decided to play cowboys and Indians. They decided to capture my mom and when they tied her up, they cut some of her hair, thinking they were scalping her."*
>
> *- Julie Sanders Culpepper (Pearl's granddaughter)*

Since it was too difficult to climb the stairs anymore, and I was nearly blind, I moved to an apartment complex for seniors in Columbus, Ohio, to be nearer to my youngest daughter, Betty, and my youngest son, Dale. They both cared for me very well indeed during my last years, along with Mary, who was living in California.

Although my life did not turn out like I had planned, the bright lights in my existence were always my children. Even though it was extremely stressful having so many of them, I was lucky that, in general, they were pretty good kids. I know that George set the house on fire twice – or maybe that was Dale who did it once – but generally the kids kept out of serious trouble.

Looking back on my life now, in my 80s, I really should have appreciated my mother and father more for taking us all in like they

Norma, Sara, Arthur, Mary, George, Pearl, Elizabeth, Dale Carter, Mount Vernon, Ohio, 1966

did. At the time, I felt that they could have given us more space to live in, but truly they were very generous to have housed us for so many years. After all, when I went out to work during the days, my mother had to keep an eye on my seven kids. I wish I had given her more thanks for doing that while she was alive.

My oldest child, Norma Deaine Carter, had to be the mama in charge when I wasn't around; and I heard from the other kids that she did the job well! She always made sure the other kids got their chores done before I got home. I felt a little guilty, though, that I gave her so much responsibility while I was away working two jobs most of my life. Norma left Mount Vernon in 1956. She moved to Cleveland, Ohio, to work in the upscale Macys department store as her career. She had one son, Jeffrey Carter, who had some mental issues, forcing him to live in halfway houses most of his life. Norma lived reasonably contentedly for many years, except for constantly worrying about Jeff. She lived companionably with a man named Ed. She had always had difficulties walking, primarily from the significant varicose veins she developed, perhaps from standing all of her life as a sales associate in department stores. Norma passed away quietly in her apartment in 2004, from heart disease and lung cancer; the latter probably caused by her lifelong smoking habit.

My second child, Sarah Carter Thomas, was a different kind of child. She always had something going on which she kept very private from the rest of the family. She was usually on the negative side too, always having something just a little "off" to say about other people. She somehow found a husband in Coley Thomas. One day in her early 20s she came downstairs with a packed suitcase and told us she was moving to Cleveland. There was no warning in advance and no invitation to the wedding. She ended up having two sons - Coley and Wilson - and made her living in Cleveland as a hairdresser. Coley Thomas Jr., like his cousin Jeff Carter, had some mental challenges, becoming a Hare Krishna[19] cult follower, then living in halfway houses, as a hermit. Sara's son, Wilson Thomas, seemed to be doing fine, marrying a woman named Katherine Beasley in 1991, but divorcing a few years later. Sara died in Cleveland, Ohio, in 1994, from metastatic adenocarcinoma (cancer) of the colon, with extensive lung involvement, according to her Death Certificate. She was so secretive, though, we never knew about her illness.

My eldest son, Arthur "Sonny" Carter, adored his automobiles, just like his daddy. He always had one or more cars parked on the lawn in front of our house, or in the street. Sonny could be quite friendly, but most of the time he was hermit-like and very private, like his sister Sara. He did not usually willingly communicate with family. Here is a true story: when Mary and her family came to visit us from California for a big family reunion in 1983, Sonny wouldn't open the door to greet us all, even though we called his name and banged on the door. We were all pretty confident that he was there, though, so we all started chatting with him from outside the house! It was kind of funny, really! Sonny had been an excellent athlete in his youth and even though his heart finally gave out in 2006, after having been short of breath for years, he was still looking fairly strong. None of us really knew much about his life or friends, and he never married nor had any children.

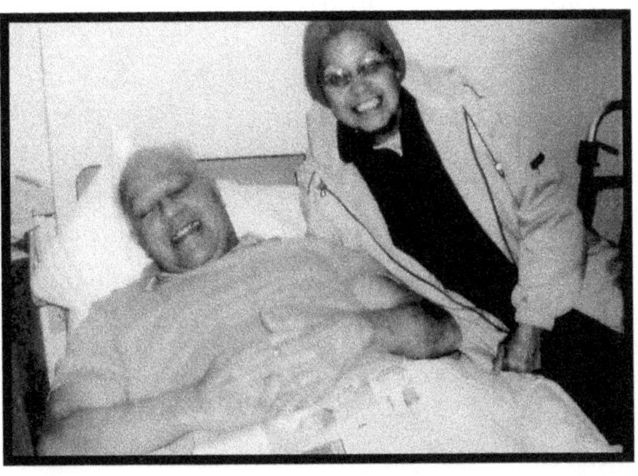

Arthur "Sonny" Carter and Elizabeth "Betty" Sanders, Hilliard, Ohio, 2006

My middle child, Mary Ellen Marshall, was very quiet like me. She was a born artist, yet was very competitive at many sports, as well as bridge. Mary confided to me that she had vowed never to be a domestic employee, nor get married before her 21st birthday. She followed through with both of her dreams, marrying Thomas Marshall at 21 and moving across country. She eventually moved to Sacramento, California, where she became a teacher, then principal. Every week, Mary and I would talk and laugh and commiserate for hours on the phone. She always made sure I had whatever I needed to be comfortable in my old age. Mary ended up having three children - Kathy, Carrie and Greg. I would regularly write letters to her daughter, Kathy, mainly talking about the scandalous happenings on the "All My Children" TV soap opera. I stayed with Mary's family during December of 1972, and never once missed not having snow!

My son George William Carter sure liked his beer and cigarettes! He was always pleasant and a hard worker, and he could build or fix anything, mechanical or otherwise. Did he get that talent from our enslaved ancestors from whom our family lore suggests could repair anything on the farm? George mainly did a lot of odd jobs during his lifetime until he got sick with varicose veins and cirrhosis of the liver. He married Tommy Driscoll and had four children - George William who was born in 1964; Tommy Gene who served in the Army between 1983 and 1987, and who died at the age of 37 in 2002; Pamula Sue who moved to Los Angeles California, and Michael Lee. Occasionally some of George's kids kept in touch with me.

My youngest daughter, Elizabeth "Betty" Carter Sanders, was always a delight, making people laugh with her sense of humor and gracious, mischievous smile. During the last years of my life, after I moved to Columbus, Ohio, Betty was my most diligent caretaker. She checked in with me several times a week, making sure I had all the daily necessities, took me to the doctor, etc. Unfortunately, I was so miserable and felt so helpless at times that I did not show Betty the appreciation she deserved for all of her kind administrations. She selflessly and cheerfully assisted me in my last dozen or so years. Of all my children, besides Dale, Betty and her kids probably kept in touch with me the most. Granddaughter Julie Sanders Culpepper and her children, Donald Junior, Kelcey, and twins Kendelle and Kamille, often called, visited, helped, and made me feel wanted and loved. Grandsons Everett - who had his mother's comedic personality - and Roy Sanders, could be counted on when something needed fixing around the house.

My youngest son, Dale Carter, was also extremely attentive to me and my needs. Dale was a likable, can-do fellow, always willing to lend a hand, and always ready to talk about current events and memories. He and Betty were a powerful team that kept me going for many years, through the dreary grey winters and the uncomfortable summers, after I very willingly gave up my "career" as a professional domestic employee. Dale had been married three times, producing a total of four children: Dale Edward and Eric Todd Carter were from his first wife, Bonnie Simpson Carter. Roger and Nicole Carter were from his third wife, Paula Myers Carter. Roger has sons Nicholas who graduated from high school with a football scholarship in 2016, Derrick born in 2008, and daughter Ava, born in 2016.

Whatever happened to that wayward husband of mine, Arthur Carter? Once my daughter Mary retired, she became obsessed with finding out what happened to him. Her last memory of him was when she was five years old and he gave her a nickel for her birthday. After some searching, Mary found her father had married a woman named Martha Carter; she divorced him in 1971 for "gross neglect of duty." I had to chuckle, hearing proof that our marital problems weren't all caused by me. Arthur's Death Certificate indicated he died on August 8, 1994, in Pittsburgh, Pennsylvania, of an acute myocardial infarction. He would have liked the fancy diagnosis!

Pearl Lavata Williams Carter, Columbus, Ohio, 1908-1990

You know, I always loved my name Pearl. It made me feel pretty and very special, like a "Pearl of great price" from the book "*The Good Earth*." I hear tell that my daddy named me Pearl after a friend of his who worked with him in East Liverpool, Ohio. Even though my life was very hard, and was not at all what I dreamed it would be, I feel gratified that I had so much love in my life, from my children and grandchildren, and the unending support of my parents.

Arthur and I enhanced this world by producing many good citizens and college graduates, including:

- Machinist/welders: Sonny, Dale and George Carter, Kathy Marshall.

- Military patriots: Dale and George Carter, Tommy and Pamula Carter, and Isaac Anderson.
- Structural and mechanical engineers: Everett Sanders III, Everett Sanders IV, and Roy Sanders; Greg Marshall does carpentry.
- Computer experts: Matthew and Isaac Anderson.
- School administrators: Mary Marshall and Carrie Malenab.
- Home decor designers: Julie Sanders Culpepper.
- Artists: Mary Ellen Marshall, Kathy "Kanika" Marshall, and Brandon Sanders.
- Hair dressers and sales: Sara Carter Thomas, Norma Carter.
- Entrepreneurs and inventors: Greg Marshall, also a firefighter.
- Analysts and researchers: Kathy Marshall.
- College graduates: Mary Marshall, Dale Carter, Kathy Marshall, Carrie Marshall Malenab, Julie Sanders Culpepper, Everett Sanders III, Roy Sanders, Greg Marshall, Alaunda Gates, Everett Sanders IV, Lauren McGhee, Matthew Anderson, Kendelle Culpepper.

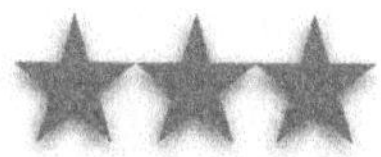

[Author's Note: Pearl Williams Carter was born in 1908 and passed away in January 1990, the same week that her granddaughter, Kathy, found out she was pregnant with her second son, Matthew Anderson. The thoughts presented in "Day's work Raised a Family" were derived from census, marriage, and divorce records, as well as documented interviews with Lavata Williams and Dale and Paula Carter, entries from Mary Marshall's journal, letters, and the author's personal knowledge of her grandmother. Whenever I am feeling low or frustrated with my life, I think of the tenacity of my grandmother Carter who persevered no matter how tired her feet were, or how worried she was about money, or how angry she may have been about her life situation. When I look around at my paid-off home and colorful garden full of my outdoor sculptures, I give homage to my ancestors who worked hard and kept their wits about them. Their sacrifices let me live wherever I want, work wherever I want, and love whomever I want.]

The Ancestors Are Smiling!

Chapter 5: The Medical Pioneer

From the Mouth of Charles Elmer Williams

Many people have heard about the questionable medical practices that have been performed on African Americans for centuries. Invasive surgeries and other shocking experiments were commonplace on slaves before the Civil War, according to some old medical journals. Electric shocks, brain surgery, amputations, as well as surgical experiments to treat injuries, birth defects, and tumors, were all pioneered on slaves, often without any pain relief in an era before anesthesia or sterile surgery.[20]

"The Immortal Life of Henrietta Lacks" is the true story about a black woman in Maryland whose immortal cancer cells, known as HeLa, were taken from her body without her knowledge. HeLa became one of the most important tools in medicine, vital in developing the polio vaccine, gene mapping, cloning, and more. Her family has not been compensated in any way for the use of their mother's cells.[21]

The Tuskegee Syphilis Project, from 1932 to 1972, was another medical project gone terribly awry. Conducted by the United Stated Public Health Service, investigators enrolled 600 impoverished, African American sharecroppers from Macon County, Alabama, of which 399 already had syphilis. After funding for treatment was lost, the study was continued without informing the men they would never be treated. They were allowed to die without the life-saving penicillin cure, while doctors studied the long-term effects of syphilis on the human body.

These are several examples of reasons why the African American public is generally leery of medical interventions.

However, what follows is the remarkable story of an untested new drug, streptomycin, which was given to a consenting African American medical pioneer in 1946. Charles Elmer Williams not only survived the disease and the treatment, but thrived, and is still living in his 90s!

Born in 1924 in Mount Vernon, Ohio, I was a typical boy who liked to play football and basketball. My friends and family also looked forward to skating on Monday nights, which was the only time black people were allowed in the skating rink. Many other businesses were segregated as well, especially restaurants like "The Alcove." My mother usually took me to the movies on Fridays, which was her day off. Like other segregated places in town, blacks were supposed to sit in specified areas. In the movie theater, "our" area was on the left side near the back. My indomitable mother, however, always sat wherever she felt like sitting and took me with her! Nobody dared say anything to Mrs. Myrtle Booker Williams, perhaps because she did laundry for many of the white people in town, or perhaps because she exuded an inner confidence that would not be challenged. She demonstrated an important lesson to me about standing up for our rights.

I had a younger brother, Robert, who was an award-winning artist and a great singer. I also had three older sisters: Reba, Pearl, and Jayne. We spent our childhood in a company-owned house at 217 North Norton Street, which my parents rented from the Cooper-Bessemer factory were my dad worked. We had large backyard with a very long porch on the front containing a porch swing and chairs.

My dad, Otho "Sherman" Williams, loved the street life: playing loud music with a band, playing cards for money, and being with his fun-loving friends. He played many musical instruments, but especially the violin and banjo. Many of us wondered how fun-loving Sherman and the serious, strict, independent, avidly-religious Myrtle Booker, ever met each other in the first place! We do know that they were both working in East Liverpool, Ohio, at the turn of the 20th century. They worked in separate private homes, where mother was a maid and daddy a driver. I seriously doubt that they met in church, as some people assumed! In fact, my mother often nagged daddy about going to church to learn the mighty word of the Lord. I remember one Sunday, mother was particularly vocal about him accompanying her. He responded, “I have no reason to go to church on Sunday because I see all the same people on Saturday night!” Somehow, their paths crossed, though, and they married in Philadelphia, Pennsylvania, in 1905, and “my” history was begun nineteen years later in 1924.

My father should have been considered and paid as an engineer at the Cooper-Bessemer machine plant where he worked. Even though he looked like a white man to some, he was not. Therefore, he was not allowed to join the Steelworker’s Union and was only allowed to perform menial jobs during the dayshift when management was around. However, engineers on the night shift always came to our house to get daddy to repair the temperamental machinery. It seemed to me that the white so-called engineers had no clue as to how to keep the machinery running. It was maddening that daddy wasn’t getting paid for his skills! At an early age, I vowed to insist on getting the job titles I deserved.

While in high school, I received extensive machine shop training and learned to make equipment tools and die. At the end of my senior year, I enrolled in the United States Navy, feeling it was my duty to help fight in World War II. The military attempted to slot me into a cook or porter job, like they did almost all other black men. However, I was a skilled machinist who successfully lobbied my case that I should be a bonafide Machinist Mate, perhaps the first black man to hold that title in the Navy. Soon, people treated me with respect, as I was doing the same precision work everyone else was doing. I guess I was a sort of pioneer in the Navy.

In 1943, I was stationed in the Great Lakes Naval Training Center near Chicago, Illinois. Then I transferred to Whitby Island, near Seattle, Washington. At both places I was a Machinist Mate, making precision parts for various types of military equipment. Like many military personnel, I always sent the majority of my paycheck back home to my mother, who diligently saved my money for me.

In 1946, during a military ceremony, while in my dress whites uniform, I fainted. I woke up some time later in a Veterans Hospital in Staten Island, New York. I found myself in a quarantined ward with ten other very sick patients. I had contracted tuberculous pneumonia. At that time, tuberculosis was nearly always a death sentence.

Tuberculosis is a disease that has plagued humankind for millennia. Even though the tubercle bacillus that causes tuberculosis was discovered by Robert Koch in 1788, there was no known cure. Many doctors were actively researching numerous treatments for this devastating disease. I did not want to die, but I was unimaginably sick. My doctors presented me with a choice to become part of an unofficial medical trial for the streptomycin antibiotic in 1946. I suppose I volunteered to be a human guinea pig of sorts, even though they could not guarantee it would keep me alive. Thankfully, I was given a chance at life and I grabbed it!

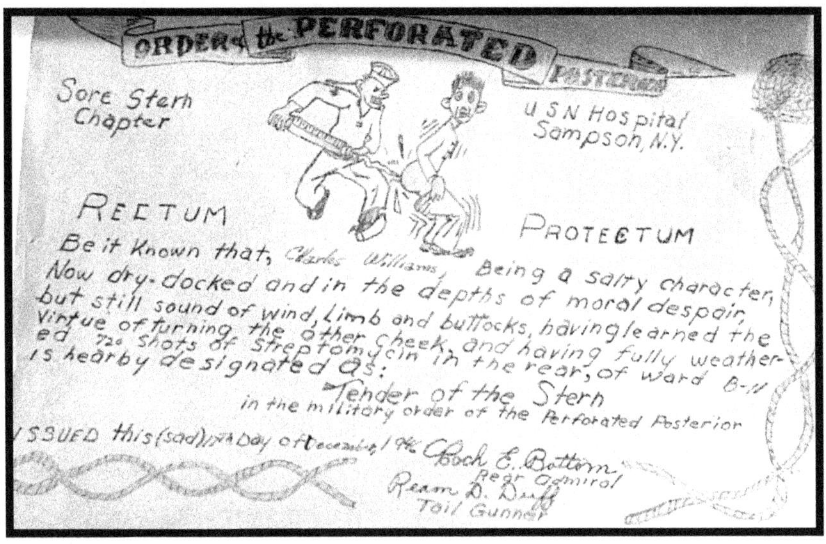

Cartoon given to Charles Williams for surviving tuberculosis, 1946

I was in the hospital for quite a while - I cannot even remember how long it was. I was poked and prodded with painful shots many times each day, for days on *end* (as shown in the cartoon). I came into the hospital weighing 180 pounds, but had deteriorated to a puny 130 pounds from the disease. After the streptomycin miracle cure, by the time I returned home to Mount Vernon, Ohio, I had returned back to 160 pounds. Yes, I was a medical pioneer and very happy to be alive!

After I came back home from being discharged, I was taking some math courses offered to veterans at Mount Vernon High School. That is where my eye caught the woman who would become my bride. Margaret Peterson and I married in 1955 in Mount Vernon, Ohio.

My dear brother, Bob, had passed away from mis-diagnosed appendicitis in 1955. The whole family mourned his loss. On top of that, jobs were difficult to come by for black people in that small center-of-Ohio town. At the advice of my sister, Jayne, we moved to Rome, New York, where she lived. Jayne was able to get me an entry-level job at Griffiths Air Force Base shredding classified documents. Yes, it was beneath my skill level, but it was a job! Once I got my foot into the Civil Service door, I could apply for a machinist job on base in 1956. My wife got a job at the Rome Cable Company. By 1957, we had two children: Delores Jean and Robert "Bob" Williams. Life was good. However, after another terrifying bout with tuberculosis in 1959, half of my left lobe (lung) was removed at the Veterans Hospital in Syracuse, New York. It took about a year to recuperate, but life went on.

We purchased our first home in Rome, New York, at 524 Millbrook Road. I used my mechanical and construction skills to build a garage, patio, and back and front porch; that house is still standing today. From 1966 to 1968, I felt a lot of personal pride in building our second family home in Rome. My mechanical skills were certainly put to the test on that project! See me there finishing up the roof?

Charles Williams Builds his family home in Rome, New York, c. 1968

Since moving to New York, I had been going to night school, earning a Bachelor of Arts degree in Education in 1968, from Oswego State University. I became a Shop Teacher at Utica Free Academy in the later 1960s through the late 1980s. I also taught Industrial Math, exposing my students to the burgeoning field of computer-aided design, retiring in 1988. We lived in Rome, New York, until about 2012, when we moved to Indianapolis to be closer to my son's family.

I am so proud of my family! My wife of 62 years has been my best friend, as well as a great mother. She retired from the Metropolitan Insurance Company in 1997. Her hobbies include gardening, playing bridge, bingo, and canasta. She also enjoys reading, played the hand

Charles, Margaret, Robert, Bob, and Corey Williams, Rome NY, c. 1986

bells, and singing in the First United Methodist Church choir.

My daughter, Delores Jean Williams, was born in Washington D.C. She went to Geneseo State University in Geneseo, NY, where she received a B.S. in Education and now teaches grammar and composition at Estancia Valley Academy in New Mexico.

My son, Bob Williams, born in 1957, enjoyed a stellar 25-year career in the U.S. Air Force, where he managed public affairs in a large variety of capacities. He was chief of the Air Force's public communication division at the Pentagon from 1998-2002, during the 9/11 attacks. Let me tell you, wondering whether my son was one of the casualties, was a time my family will never forget! Bob was also the director of public affairs for the Air Force Flight Test Center at Edwards Air Force Base (1996-98), chief of the external relations division for Germany-based U.S. Air Forces in Europe (1993-96), and chief of media relations in the Air Force's office in New York (1988-91). Bob retired as a colonel in 2004. In 2005, he joined the National Collegiate Athletic Association as vice president of communications, and he served on several advisory boards in Indiana. Bob has two sons, Robert and Corey with his first wife, Gina Sachs. In 2015, Bob found love again and married Linda Johnson in Wilkinson, Indiana. I am in my 93rd year writing this story: a true medical miracle!

[Author's Note: I am so pleased to have been able to speak with all three of our oldest living Williams relatives for this book (Charles, Lavata, Dale) for they lived with the patriarch of the family, Otho Sherman Williams, and can provide the clearest picture of how life was for our family in the 1900s.]

The ancestors are smiling!

Chapter 6: Family Photographs

2003 Family Reunion in Columbus, Ohio

Joseph Booker Family

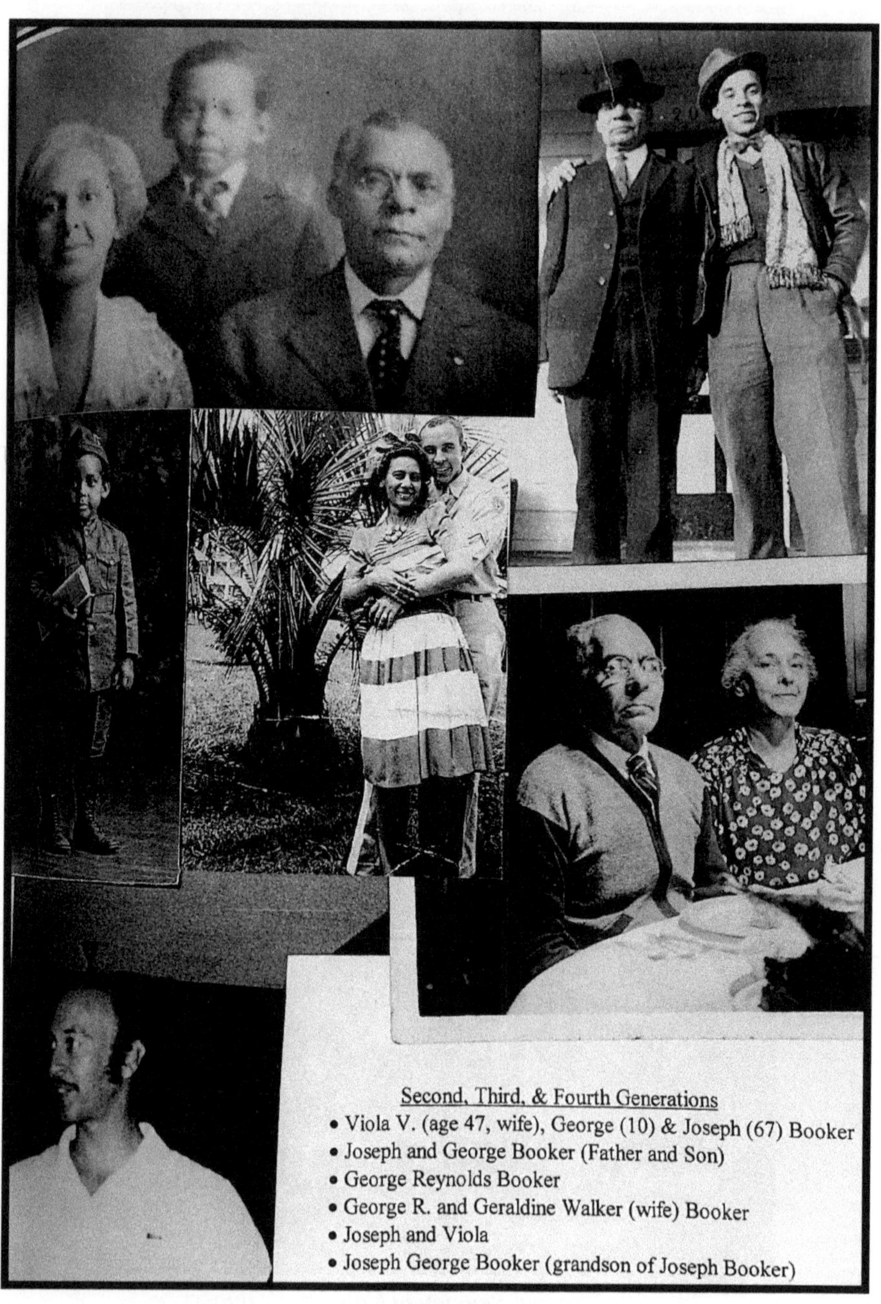

Second, Third, & Fourth Generations

- Viola V. (age 47, wife), George (10) & Joseph (67) Booker
- Joseph and George Booker (Father and Son)
- George Reynolds Booker
- George R. and Geraldine Walker (wife) Booker
- Joseph and Viola
- Joseph George Booker (grandson of Joseph Booker)

Booker Family Life - Early-to-Mid 1900s

Reba May and Myrtle "Lavata" Williams Family

<u>Sixth and Seventh Generation</u>

•Reba Williams at 9 months and around 43.

•M. Lavata Williams (daughter) at 18 and around 54.

•On a Mediterranean cruise to Greece, Egypt, Israel, & Turkey.1977

Jayne Elizabeth Williams Family

Jayne Elizabeth Williams Prince and Gates Family
Seventh Generation
Saundra (Myers/ Gates) Fort
Courtland Craig Prince Jr. (1983)
Sixth Generation
Jayne (Williams) Prince
& Courtland Prince (husband)
Eight Generation
Alaunda Elaina Gates
Leaunda Jayne (Gates) Durax
Thomas Edward Gates
D'Lisa Danielle Fort
Courtland Craig Prince III
Jason Dion Prince
Launi
Joelle
Sauni

Charles Elmer Williams Family

Margaret Peterson   Charles Elmer Williams

Delores Jean Williams

Linda Johnson   Robert Charles Williams

Robert Charles Williams   Corey James Williams

Pearl Lavata Williams Carter Family, page 1

Pearl Lavata Williams Carter

Sara Elizabeth Carter

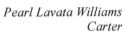

Sarah Lavata (Carter), & sons, Coley Jr. & Wilson Thomas

Norma Deaine & son Jeffrey Lewis Carter

Arthur Lewis Carter (Sunny)

Norma and Jeff Carter Family Arthur "Sonny" Carter

Pearl Lavata Williams Carter Family, page 2

Mary Ellen Marshall Family

Matthew Anderson · *Greg Marshall* · *Ken Anderson* · *Kathy & Matt Marshall Anderson* · *Lauren McGhee* · *Mary Marshall* · *Isaac Anderson*

Carrie and Romeo Malenab, Lauren McGhee, and E'Drece Walls, 2016

Jameillah, Jeremiah, Isaac, Jazmine, Isaiah Anderson, 2017

Pearl Lavata Williams Carter Family, page 3

George William Carter Family

George Williams (top) 1936-2003
George W. Jr. and Tommy Géan Jr.
Pamula Sue Michael Lee Williams

Pearl Lavata Williams Carter Family, page 4
Elizabeth "Betty" Carter Sanders Family

Sanders-Culpepper Family
Back: Don Jr., Kendelle, Kelcey & Kamille Culpepper, Maysa, Brandon, Aisha
Front: Dom Culpepper, William, Benson, Everett II (seated), and Sephora Sanders

Paula and Roy Sanders

Elizabeth "Betty" Carter Sanders

Everett III and Lynnette Sanders

Jasmine and Everett Sanders IV

Don and Julie Culpepper

Pearl Lavata Williams Carter Family, page 5
Dale Edward Carter Family

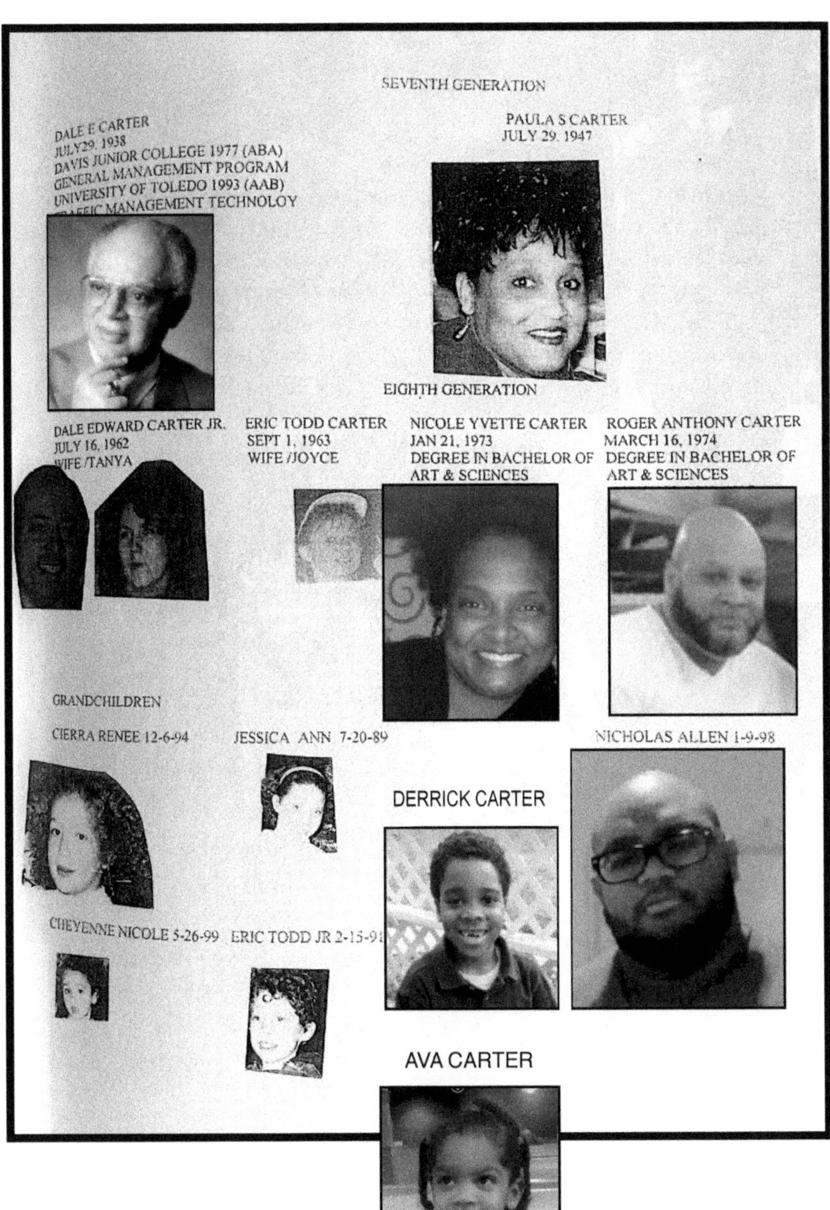

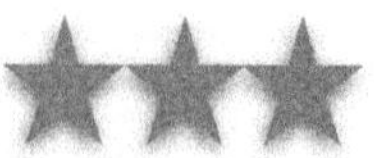

[Author's Note: The family photographs on the previous pages were initially included in a 2003 Family History booklet prepared by Lavata Williams for a family reunion in Columbus, Ohio. That reunion was chaired by her cousins Dale Carter and Betty Carter Sanders and Betty's daughter Julie Sanders Culpepper. Where available, photographs were updated and new generations were added for this 2017 book.]

Chapter 7: The Designated Genealogist

From the Mouth of Myrtle Lavata Williams

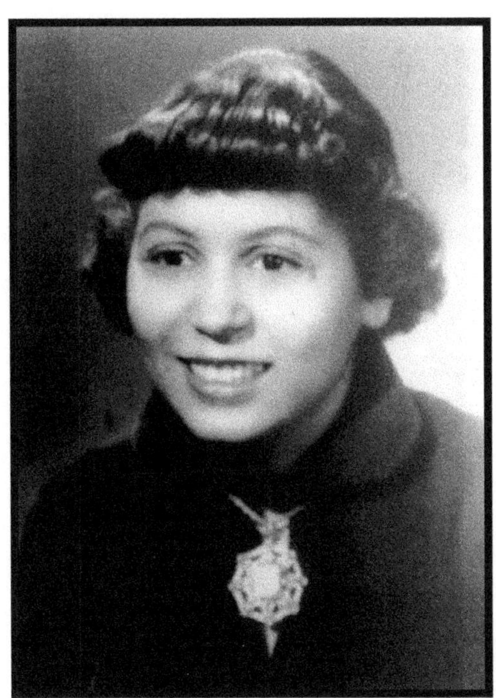

"We have had four family reunions since the 1980s. I don't remember any before that - family gatherings certainly - but not reunions. The first was in 1983, in Mansfield, Ohio, at the lovely Mohican State Park resort. This was when Lauren McGhee, my first grandchild, was 18 months old. About 80 to 100 people attended this reunion, and a whole new side of the family was present! The second reunion was in Old Sacramento, California, in 1986, with about 30 members. A third was a really mini reunion during the summer of 1997 in Sacramento. The last one was in 2003 in Columbus, Ohio."

- Mary Ellen Marshall, "Reflections from a Mother's Heart"

Many people become genealogists because they love history. Some love the challenge of piecing together historical puzzles and solving problems. Some desperately want to know where their family came from and where they fit into the universe. Sometimes people become genealogists purely by happenstance: that rather describes me, Myrtle "Lavata" Williams, the dutiful daughter who became a designated genealogist. Oh, you have never heard that expression before? Well let me explain what it is and how it all happened.

I was the only child of Reba May Williams (1907-2014). You probably already heard about my mother NOT receiving her high school diploma in 1925, because she stubbornly refused to complete one assignment, so I won't repeat her entire story here (even though it was so exciting to see all the international newspaper, magazine and TV press she received at the age of 106!) My mother left her childhood home in Mount Vernon, Ohio, to do day's work for the Hairston Family in Columbus, Ohio. Her days were spent cleaning, doing a little light cooking and their laundry. After a couple of years, though, an unplanned pregnancy brought her back home to Mount Vernon, to give birth to me in November 1933. She never told me the particulars of what happened in Columbus or who my father was.

After I was born, my mother worked as a housekeeper for various white families in town. Then, thank the Lord! The biggest break in our lives came in 1942! Mother got the job of a lifetime working as a "second girl" in the home of Pulitzer Prize winning author, Louis Bromfield, in his beautiful Malabar Farm in Lucas, Ohio. I went with her to live there when I was nine years old. Soon thereafter, the primary Malabar Farm cook did not show up for work and mother filled in. She performed well enough that she was offered the permanent job! Mother cooked for about 20 people every day, and that included the Bromfield family and the farm hands. When there were large parties, though, Mr. B - that's what mother called Mr. Bromfield - had the event catered. One of the biggest events there was the marriage of movie stars Humphrey Bogart and Lauren Bacall, and we were invited to attend!

During the week, I went to school in the lush, rural, Lucas Valley schools with the other children living on farms and ranches throughout the valley. Occasionally, I was driven to the all-white school by Mr. B's chauffeur, but I usually took the bus along the winding and forested roads. Life was very lonely for me because I was the only young person at Malabar Farm, and my school friends lived miles away in that rural community. They were almost like family to me.

I must share with you a very important experience that happened to me in 1952, when my high school graduating class went on a field trip to Washington DC. At that time, the capital of the United States of America was entirely segregated, with "white only" signs everywhere. When we arrived in DC in May, the tour bus met us at the train station. I could not stay in the hotel with the rest of my class, though, because I was a Negro. I was taken by limousine to a hotel for black people; however, at 10 PM, Mrs. Fairy, our teacher, and her son removed me from that hotel because it was known for prostitution.

They took me instead to Phyllis Wheatley, a room-and-board house for single black women. The white tour bus driver was very nice to me, and would come each morning to bring me to the hotel to have breakfast with my classmates. Since Negroes were not allowed in that hotel, special arrangements had to be made for our class to have meals in a private room, so I could eat with my class, unseen by others. The bus driver would take my classmates to the hotel at night, then me back to Phyllis Wheatley. Sometimes the driver would take me sightseeing in DC to and from picking up my other classmates. I remember that my class friends were absolutely appalled, dismayed, saddened, and just plain mad at the treatment I received in Washington DC, our nation's capital! In little Lucas Valley, Ohio, I was the only black person in the school, yet I was always treated with respect, just like a regular person, because that's who I was!

Really, my school friends were more like family. Sometimes we seemed to do more socializing than learning though! Being an only child, I have maintained lasting relationships for 70 years with many of my school chums. My schoolmate, Bud, would get us together several times a year to reminisce and enjoy each other's company. Everyone was devastated when Bud died last year, right before we were to have our get annual get-together, but the rest of us vowed to stay in touch.

Every summer between the ages of nine and 18, I was able to reconnect with my grandparents and cousins while living in Granddad and Grandmother Williams' crowded house in Mount Vernon, Ohio. Up to 16 people often lived in their two-story, white clapboard house. My first cousin, Mary Carter, was my best friend during those eventful summer months. We would pick dandelion, collard and mustard greens, place them in large baskets, and sell them to neighbors to make some pocket money. What I remember most, though, is laughing and having fun with my family.

The summer of 1947 was extremely enlightening. Mary and I were given the task of entertaining Granddad Williams. He had dementia and we had to keep him from walking to his former job every day. During that summer, we learned a bit about his and Grandmother William's lives, but not much about his enslaved Williams ancestors. When my Mary's daughter, Kathy Marshall, asked me questions about our enslaved Williams family in Maryland, there wasn't much I could tell her. Although I did profess that I believe we get our mechanical and problem solving abilities from our enslaved ancestors. According to family lore, Great-Grandpa Booker and perhaps Great-Granddad Williams, both slaves in the mid-1800s, had to repair the equipment on their respective plantations. We have so many people in our family who either work directly with metal as machinists, or are fix-it people, or are good at planning, organizing and implementing activities that solve problems. Were those skills genetically passed down by our enslaved ancestors who had to figure out how to survive during slavery?

After graduating from high school in 1952, I worked part-time as an elevator operator at Rudin's Department Store, then as a switchboard operator. I also handled invoices for merchandise at Ringwalt's Department store. I attempted a couple of semesters at Ohio State University, but I was not prepared for the rigors of college.

Hmmm, so what was I going to do with my life? I decided to enroll in Mount Vernon Business College, majoring in accounting, while still working at Ringwalt's. I liked working with numbers, so I got a job as a Junior Accountant for the City of Columbus, Ohio. Now feeling more independent, I decided to move to Washington D.C. in 1964 and work as an accounting technician there. I also took classes to prepare me to enroll in Teacher's College. I knew I wanted to work with children and help them prepare for the world before them, so I majored in Elementary Education.

Can you imagine being on your own in the nation's capital, living in a boarding house with several other women, all eating together in the dining room, all sharing stories at the table? Can you imagine being able to visit the many historical and cultural sites in D.C. and going to museums on your lunch break? Well, I absolutely loved every minute of it! Some said I was a looker with attractive physical characteristics and I soon attracted the attention of a particular man - a man who very much wanted to marry me. The stickler was that he was an East Indian whose parents would not approve of him marrying anyone outside their ethnicity. I was uncomfortable with the thought that I would not be accepted by his family, so I terminated the relationship and continued on my independent way.

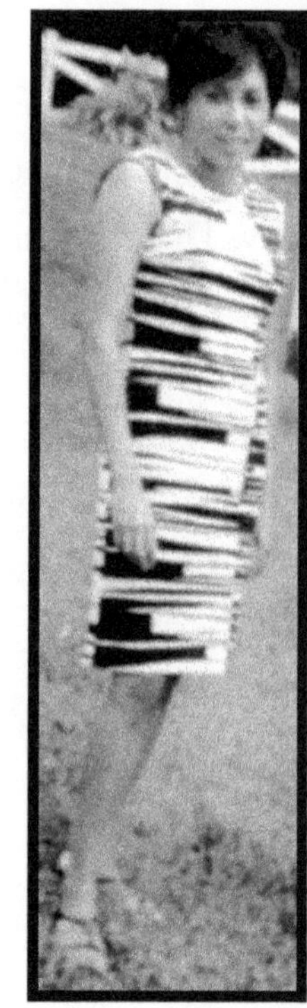

Lavata Williams D.C.. c. 1970

From 1964 to 1971, I worked for the Federal Government as an Accounting Technician. Unfortunately, I experienced several negative encounters with the local black coworkers there who did not want a "yellow" skinned woman from the North (Ohio) taking their job. During this very stressful period, I volunteered to work with the Congress of Racial Equality (CORE)[22] to help teach young minority children to read. I really felt I was making a big difference in their lives, so I worked hard to earn a teaching credential. I moved back to Columbus, Ohio, to teach first through fifth grade children, until I retired in 1995.

So how did I get to be the designated genealogist? Well, the elders of our family came to visit me and mother one afternoon in the summer of 1982. My mother and Aunt Pearl Carter, and their first cousin Joanna Walker, said "Lavata, these younger children don't even know they are cousins. They could pass each other on the street and not know they are even related! Lavata, we elders designate you to arrange a big family reunion next summer. You will invite all the family members and you will get them to attend the reunion." Back then, younger people did not question adults, even a 39-year-old, like me. I nodded my head yes in acknowledgement and proceeded to carry out their mandate. My love of history prompted me to take it upon myself to document our family tree and give each family a copy of my research at the reunion the following year, which was a mere 12 months away. I became a "Designated Genealogist." When the elders tell you to do something, you do it without asking questions.

How in the world did I do all of that in what seemed like only a few months, mostly by myself? Because I am a very organized person, it was pretty easy for me. I created a work plan, contacted Mohican State Park Lodge and Conference Center, and reserved it for three days for our family reunion in July 1983.

Mohican State Park Lodge and Conference Center, 1983

Then I took a genealogy class to find out how to collect family history information. Next, I sent letters to all family members telling them about the reunion and how to reserve rooms, how to provide information about their family birth and death dates, etc., and to return the information to me no later than October 1982. I interviewed the family elders and took notes from their oral history about our family relationships. Remember, this was before the age of computers, so I had

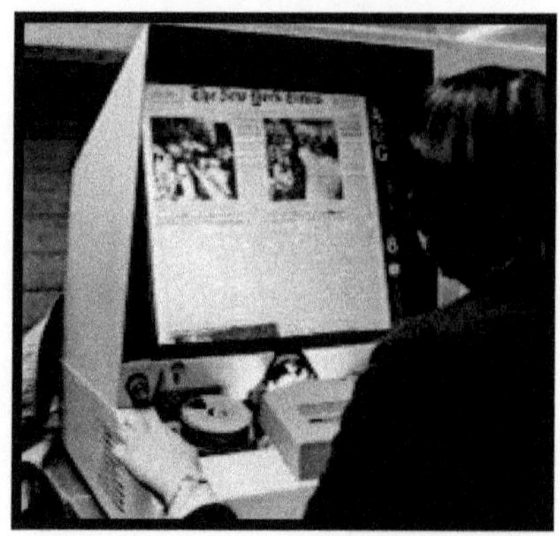

Microfilm reader

to laboriously search census records using a microfilm reader to confirm the oral histories. I researched census and other records and visited cemeteries in Mount Vernon and Barnesville, Ohio, where many of our family lived, to ensure the elders' stories were true. Then I typed all the information using a manual typewriter, made numerous copies, and assembled 22 pages of birth, death and marriage information, by family, by generation into family history binders for each family. In addition, I included a few family stories. It's pretty simple if you are an organized person!

```
                    Sixth Generation

William Booker Scott B: June, 1899, Ill. D: unk
  M: unk.  C: Barbar Scott, brothers' names unk.

Reba May Williams B: Jan. 23, 1907, Phil. Pa.  C: Myrtle L

Pearle Lavata Williams B: Oct. 7, 1908, Phil. Pa.
  M: Arthur Taft Carter,                Mt. Vernon, Oh.
     B: May 2, 1908, Mt. Vernon, Oh. D: unk
  C: Norma D., Sara L., Arthur L., Mary E., George W.
     Elizabeth A., Dale E.

Jayne E. Williams B: July 23, 1920, Mt. Vernon, Oh.
  M: Paul P. Myers, Dec. 1939, Marion, Oh
     B: Sept. 1918, Mt. Vernon, Oh. D: 1976, Mt. Vernon, Oh.
     C: Saundra L.
  M: Courtland C. Prince Sr., Dec 22, 1946, Dayton, Oh.
     B: Sept. 26, 1919, Dayton, Oh. C: Courtland C. Jr.
```

Sample page in Lavata Williams' 1983 Family Reunion Binder

My Uncle George Booker, a gregarious and well-liked postal carrier, was the moderator for the "Booker, Jenkins, Thomas, Williams" family reunion in July 1983. Each attendee was provided with a color-

Top: Flora Walker, George Booker, Geraldine Booker, Pearl and Reba Williams
Bottom: Reba, Lavata and Jayne Williams Prince, Lavata Williams, 1983

coded name tag and each family received a color-coded family history binder with my well-researched genealogy information. During our first reunion meeting that day, Uncle George told family stories, as well as the history of blacks in Mount Vernon, Ohio, where most of us lived.

We broke bread in the dining room, which had large picture windows that looked onto the white-barked birch trees that swayed gracefully in the breeze. Many attendees were meeting family members for the first time. We spent three blissful days in each other's company. The younger kids enjoyed going to the rustic rooms of the elders to hear the sometimes raucous stories of their youth. Hiking in the lush woods surrounding the complex, swimming in the clear blue waters of the L-shaped pool, and playing basketball among the trees, were among the many outdoor activities. The laughter and camaraderie forged new, or renewed old relationships, which we all vowed to continue (and which many of us did). I was pleased at how the reunion turned out and was rewarded by the elders with a nod of the head and a big smile.

Some of the family reunion attendees at Mohican State Park, Ohio, 1983

We had a few more, much smaller, family reunions after the big one in 1983. In 2003 my first cousin, Betty Carter Sanders, spearheaded a family reunion in Columbus, Ohio, with the help of her brother, Dale Carter, and me. In 1986 and 1997, my cousin Mary had a reunion, inviting Williams descendants from Ohio, as well as those who had already moved to California. It was the first time some of us had ever seen California. It makes me feel very proud to have been the first to carry out the ancestor's call to record their stories. Genealogy is certainly not my entire life though.

I always wanted to travel the world, since history is my true passion. My first trip was by myself, within the United States, traveling on passenger trains from Ohio, to Colorado, to Las Vegas, and on to visit family in San Bernardino and Los Angeles, then traveling up the California coast.

My second trip was a Middle Eastern cruise in 1979, sponsored by the National Education Association (NEA). My 70+ year-old mother and I flew into Athens, Greece, joined the NEA travel group, then toured the Parthenon and Acropolis, marveling at the millennia-years-old buildings and stone carvings that we had only read about in history books. We boarded a cruise ship and sailed to Alexandria, Egypt, then took a bus to experience the incredible pyramids and museums which had, literally, beds of gold. From there, we sailed to Israel and saw the Wailing Wall and other sacred sites we had read about in the Bible. The ship then took us to Ephesus, Turkey, to view the Library, other antiquities, and colored murals that were so well preserved we could almost imagine people still living there. A bus trip took us north to Istanbul, where we stood at the precise point where Asia, Europe, and Africa meet. I still get shivers when I think about that part of the trip. You see, we were warned many times to travel in groups of four or five, or we might be kidnapped and sold into slavery. But there were so many interesting vendors with lovely items for sale, that I walked toward one table to see a scarf. All of a sudden, a bunch of local men surrounded me and started moving me away from my group! Thankfully, one of my traveling companions noticed what was going on and quickly came to my side, pretending to be a relative. Just as quickly, the men disappeared and I was saved from a life of unspeakable horror! It took me a while to recover from the fright. Our last stop on the cruise was the beautiful Greek island of Santorini.

In the 1980s, mother and I flew to England, took a ferry to France with friends of ours, then drove around France, Italy, Spain, Germany, and Belgium over a five-week period. I have always maintained that I could happily live from a suitcase, just traveling the world enjoying history and other cultures. Even with all of the social problems in this country, I still feel blessed to be American!

Kathy Marshall, Trey Gates, Lavata Williams, Launi Gates, Carrie Malenab, Jayne Gates, Hayward, CA, 2016
The Gates are Jayne Williams Prince's grandchildren

I documented our Myers family back to Germany, and our enslaved Booker family to Virginia, but I knew nothing about my direct-line Williams ancestors. I could only remember that granddad's father was named Otho Williams, that he and his father were both born in Maryland in the 1800s, and that the elder Otho was a slave. That's all. My niece Kathy chose to attempt to uncover information about my Williams family line, relying on technology, while I did it the traditional way using microfilm and a manual typewriter. In any event, when the ancestors speak, we listen!

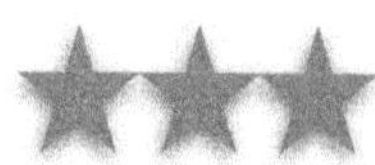

[Author's Note: M. Lavata Williams is living in a Senior Complex in Columbus, Ohio, and is enjoying a carefree life socializing with friends and attending Bible study classes.]

The ancestors are smiling!

Chapter 8: The Principal Artist

From the Mouth of Mary Ellen Marshall

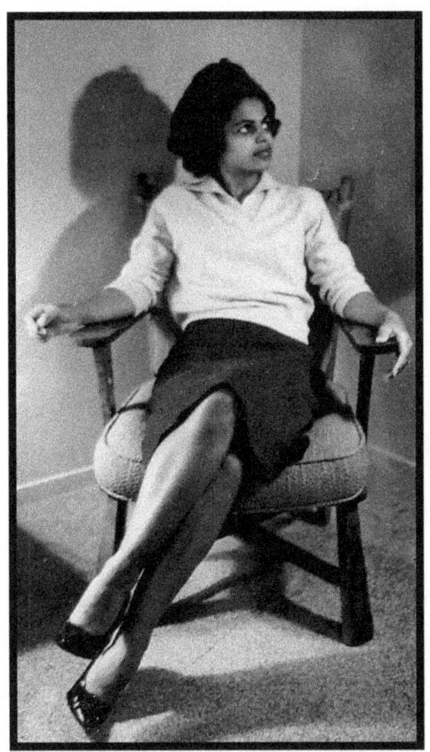

I grew up in the middle of Ohio, 13 miles from a town called Centerburg. We had lots and lots of severe winter storms! We always had to walk to school from first grade through 12th. Some days it was so blustery you couldn't see your hand! Some days the snow was so high you had to lift your feet up to your chest! Sometimes it was so slushy, icy, and slippery, it was just dangerous to be outside – but we always went to school! I do not remember any time that was worse than the worst. It was just part of life and we lived through it as though it was natural.

- Mary Ellen Marshall "Reflections from a Mother's Heart"

On Easter Sunday, April 1, 1934, I was born in Mount Vernon, Ohio. It was also April Fools Day. I was born almost exactly one hundred years after my enslaved great-grandfather Otho Williams was born in Maryland in 1834. I was the middle of seven children who were raised by our capable mother, Pearl Lavata Williams Carter. The oldest child was Norma Deaine; she had to be the second mother regarding discipline, because my mother always had to work. Sara, the second oldest, had a different way of thinking; rarely was she in the agreement mode, for she always brought in negative thoughts. Arthur, who most people called Sonny, was a wonderful athlete; whatever he did - ball games, tennis, skating - he did effortlessly. I was the fourth born; generally quiet, but also very competitive and artistic. George was the brother who thought differently, like Sara; at Christmastime, he was never satisfied with his gifts. Elizabeth, our "Betty," was always the helper and always ready to do something for someone else to make their situation better. Dale was the youngest; always a nice person who was able to survive well with the rest of us.

My father, if you could call him that, was Arthur Taft Carter. Sadly, he was rarely around, except … to make another baby. I feel that I never had a father in my life. I remember meeting him only once when I was five, at Grammie Ella Carter's house - his Mother's home.

I remember it vividly: he gave me a nickel! That is the extent of "me and my father." He was gone all the time except to produce eight children in nine years (one boy did not survive). By the time I came along, he was never there. I heard he was in jail a lot of that time, but I don't remember what he did to get jail time. I, to this day, do not know whether he is alive or dead. He just disappeared over the past 50 or so years. I do not know what kind of work he did, or for how long.

My mother, on the other hand, was my hero. She worked tirelessly doing "day's work," cleaning other peoples' homes all of her life to keep food on the table for our large family. I knew at an early age that I would not be stuck in that small town where the only jobs for black women were as a housekeeper, janitor, laundress or cook. I vowed not to get married until I was 21, and not to have a ton of babies that would limit my options for the future! Yes, I was driven to have a different sort of life.

Pearl Carter, Mount Vernon, Ohio, 1945

Growing up, I had two childhood homes located in Mount Vernon, which is in the center of Ohio, amongst the cornfields. About 17,000 people live there now, with only 191 being of African descent.[23] I don't think the minuscule percentage of black residents was much different back in the 1930s to 1950s when I was growing up there. Blacks were not concentrated in any one area, though, as we lived throughout the city.

It was good that my family lived in a small town. It helped mom rear the seven of us with fewer problems. She could leave us during the day while she worked, and we were safe. The neighbors were nosey and told mom everything we were doing. Mom would get a peach tree switch before coming into the house to spank the butts that needed it!

My preference would have been to live in a larger place, though, where opportunities for jobs would have been better. We did not leave Mount Vernon during my young years except to go to the State Fair or for occasional shopping trips in Columbus, the state Capitol, which was about 45 minutes away. This left me pretty naïve. I do remember going to Cleveland in the late 1940s to see the Cleveland Indians and Larry Doby; it was a double header and oh so thrilling!

If I had to describe my childhood bedroom, you probably wouldn't believe it! We were a family of seven, eight including my mother. All of us kids slept in the same 12' x 12' bedroom and we did this for the first 15 years of my life! In a double bed was Norma, George, Sonny, and me. In a crib, later a daybed, was Betty and Dale. Sarah slept on the floor on a pallet because she wet the bed a lot. Mom had a single bed in our kitchenette. The breeze had a hard time coming through the two windows that were at an angle on adjacent walls. We did not have a good view, but the peach tree was right outside our window at the front of the house. We would sometimes sneak out that window, climb out on the porch roof, slip down the side pole, and play outside. Later, we moved to a larger house. From age 15 to 21, we had 2 1/2 bedrooms for all of us: such a luxury of space! There were two double beds in our room which housed all four girls and we had a closet that was about 3 feet wide for all of us girls. Can you imagine?

In Mount Vernon, Ohio, I attended the Fourth Ward school as a first through sixth grader. No kindergarten was available. It was about one and a half miles from my house. We walked to school, because there was never any other way. We walked up the street in front of our house to Sandusky Street, then we walked past the Cooper-Bessemer Steel Plant, which was a really long block, then we turned right at the light and walked to the school. My junior and senior high schools were in the same building, just at opposite ends. That building was even closer to our second home; however, we had to walk up a steep hill to that school. In bad weather, snowy weather, icy weather, it was all very difficult. But Mount Vernon was a small town and this was the advantage: everything was close by. All of our schools were nice, in a good area, and the education I now know was excellent.

We really enjoyed summer activities, like playing baseball in the street. I played tennis with a black rubber ball and a stick, at the park down the street, before I got a real tennis racket. I was also a demon with marbles and loved to skate. I was competitive at so many things, even though I was a rather shy child. I was the middle child, so I guess I felt the need to excel in some way.

Mary Carter playing tennis, Mount Vernon, Ohio, c. 1950

We had a terribly frightening experience during my childhood. I turned the corner one day walking home to see our house on fire! Younger brother Dale had put lit matches in a hole in the kitchen wall to see what would happen. It was a terrible experiment! We had to stay with Aunt Vy and Uncle George Booker until our house could be rebuilt. Aunt Edna Carter also took some of us in. The house burned a second time too, but I think that was from brother George playing around with matches. Boys!

Every week for a year, I helped my mom clean Dr. Harmsted's dental offices after dinner, but my life wasn't all work and no play. After cleaning the doctor's offices, I went to the movies with mom on Fridays to watch the black and white "serials."[24] We couldn't wait to see what happened in the serial from the week before! I would also go downtown with my cousin Lavata when she visited us on some weekends from her home at Malabar Farm. We giggled and had fun all the time with each other!

My mom was calm, even when she was going out to get a peach switch to spank our butts. That's a special talent - being calm (not spanking our rears!). She didn't scream or yell. Our mornings were calm, which is an important way to start the day, especially when there are so many children around. There is no reason to have a noisy, drama-filled household. I transferred that calmness to my home when I was an adult. I made sure that we were never a family who yelled all the time or verbally abused each other.

When I was growing up, we were not like children nowadays who expect their parents to give them money for movies, video games, candy, clothes, etc. We had to earn whatever little money we had. Brothers George and Sonny caddied golf and bowling tournaments. Betty cleaned houses. Norma always worked at Rudin's, the top-notch department store in Mount Vernon. Secretive Sara always had a little something she did on the side, usually cleaning houses, I think. Dale was too young to work, but he sometimes found pennies in the street; back in the day, a penny could buy a couple of pieces of candy!

My first job was babysitting the Robert boys. They were one and two years old when I started babysitting them. I earned 25 whole cents an hour! Their mother golfed, played bridge, and partied all day and many nights. Believe me, I was there a lot. I cannot imagine leaving my kids for the long hours that she did, because I was only 11 or 12 years old myself! My next job was cleaning a family's home after school, doing "day's work" like my mother. They were very nice people and always had a clean house. I simply kept it cleaner! It was then that I knew for sure that I would do everything in my power to better myself, so that I would not have a life of cleaning other peoples' houses, as my mom had to do her whole life. This gave me the early incentive to work harder, and to do better, at whatever I encountered.

For Thanksgiving, turkeys were given to us poor folks by people who were kind. I loved turkey, dressing, cranberry sauce, pumpkin and apple pie, and mashed potatoes. Mom went all out for Thanksgiving dinner. I remember one Thanksgiving season when dad's mother, Grammie Carter, had a live turkey for several months. We got to know this bird. When it was time to kill it for Thanksgiving, its neck was wrung and he was prepared to eat. Well, I remember I could not eat that turkey. I was not from a farm and this was very sad for me to see!

Growing up, we got a tree on Christmas Eve when they were giving them away. Those trees may not have been straight or big - maybe pretty similar to the spindly one in "A Charlie Brown Christmas"[25] - but mom always had shiny bulbs to make it beautiful. There were seven stockings that mom put nuts and candy in, for that was our very favorite present. There usually wasn't any more than that, and the tree was taken down before New Years Day. When my kids were little, I had to find places to hide multiple gifts! I liked it more when my kids were teenagers and we all could enjoy Christmas without the Santa mania.

We always celebrated birthdays in our house growing up. We did that simply by having a cake made by our mother and singing happy birthday. I don't think we usually bought or made each other gifts. My very favorite birthday was when I was 18. I got some luggage and actually had a party. I think it was just family who came, but it was also around graduation time, so we really enjoyed ourselves!

Besides my mother, my junior high school art teachers, Mr. Loomis and Mrs. Lewis, shaped my life. Even so, the most memorable advice I remember getting was from a Mr. Colbert who was willing to critique my artwork. He lived in Zanesville, about an hour from my home. I would mail him some of my work, he would critique it, then mail me other art projects to complete. It was great! This communication had two major benefits: first, it kept me constructively busy as a teenager, as I could easily stay home and practice my drawing. Second, it supported me so much emotionally and financially to be able to draw! I used my artistic abilities to good advantage in high school, and certainly have used them in my senior years. I have very successfully sold my watercolor artwork during retirement. Art keeps me active, alert, energized and creative! I thoroughly enjoy being an artist, and it all started with my art teachers and a helpful guy from Zanesville, Ohio.

I was athletic, artistic, and VERY competitive at everything growing up, especially contract bridge, tennis and golf. Even though shy, I was selected to be the Art Editor for the 1952 Mount Vernon High School Yearbook - the first black student selected for that role. Additionally, even though I was a real tomboy, I was selected to become the first black female to be in the Queen's Court in high school!

My dream job came at the age of 15, working at J. S. Ringwalt's Department Store, Mount Vernon's second best department store. I trimmed the windows,[26] planned and designed them, and worked with another fellow after school to change the window vignettes each week. This meant changing clothes on the mannequins, making signs

In this Forum of the class of 1952 we are using Latin as our theme. It has been carried out in the cover and in the sketches done by Mary Ellen Carter.

Mary Carter, Art Editor for the 1952 Yearbook

MaryCarter first black in the Queen's Court
Source: 1952 Mount Vernon High School Yearbook

throughout the store, doing advertising work, and other duties, if needed. I had that job from 15 until I was 21 and left to be married. I only made 25 cents an hour, but I did get to take advantage of store sales to make my money go further.

I happily left my hometown to marry the man of my dreams, Thomas Richard Marshall, who I met in 1952. He was going to Ohio State Medical School when we met, quite unexpectedly, on a car ride to a skating rink in Zanesville, Ohio. After that initial encounter, we continued the relationship via letters. His letters were beautifully written in a fancy script and his words were loving, with a lot of thought. We saw each other sparingly, since Cleveland was 130 miles away and he had no car. This scenario was what a young girl dreams about: a very nice, handsome, tall young man, who is pursuing life with a plan of action, and who does not waste time doing worthless things like smoking, and drinking, etc. The relationship grew as time passed!

I can't remember exactly the way his marriage proposal went, but we were in Cleveland, Ohio, when I received my "Perfect" one and one-quarter diamond gold ring. I still wear the diamond on a necklace, even now in retirement. Tom took lots of pride in this ring! I knew all along that I would marry him, if he asked. I learned in Mount Vernon what I *didn't* want in a guy; there was little opportunity to learn the opposite! So when Tom came along, and he really wanted me, I knew it was meant to be. Love had come my way! We were married by a Justice of the Peace one month after my 21st birthday, on May 7, 1955. I wore a two-piece beige cotton suit that I had sewn. Tom's sister, Jean, was my maid of honor.

Mary Carter and Thomas Marshall,1953, Kappa Alpha Psi Dance

Mr. Thomas Richard Marshall and
Miss Mary Ellen Carter

MARRIAGE LICENSE APPLICATION No. 7319

To the Honorable Judge of the Probate Court of said County:

The undersigned respectfully make...... application for a Marriage License for said parties, and upon oath state:

That said Thomas Richard Marshall *is* 23 *years of age, on the* 2nd *day of* May *19* 54,
his residence is Columbus, Ohio, Franklin County,
his place of birth is Cleveland, Cuyahoga,County, Ohio,
his occupation is student,
his father's name is Austin Henry Marshall,
his mother's maiden name was Daisy Dooley,
that he was not *previously married and that he has no wife living.*

Case No. ...... *State and County* ......

That said Mary Ellen Carter *is* 21 *years of age, on the* 1st *day of* April *19* 55
her residence is Mount Vernon, *Knox County, Ohio*
her place of birth is Mount Vernon, Knox County, Ohio,
her occupation is J. S. Ringwalt Company,
her father's name is Arthur Carter,
her mother's maiden name was Pearl Williams,
that she was not *previously married*
and is ...... *her maiden name being* ......
and that she has no husband living.

Case No. ...... *State and County* ......

For record of further divorces See Page...... **Sec.**......

That neither of said parties is an habitual drunkard, epileptic, imbecile, or insane, and is not under the influence of any intoxicating liquor or narcotic drug. Said parties are not nearer of kin than second cousins; and there is no legal impediment to their marriage.

It is expected that Russell E. Lamm, Justice of the Peace *is to solemnize the marriage of said parties.*

Sworn to before me and signed in my presence, this 29th *day of* April *19* 55

[illegible] *Probate Judge*
By [illegible] *Deputy Clerk*

Thomas Richard Marshall
Mary Ellen Carter

Marriage License Application, April 29, 1955

We rented a tiny room from Bishop Allen, pastor at the A.M.E. Church, but he and his wife never believed we were actually married and treated us almost like heathen criminals for the 30 days we stayed with them! There was no honeymoon because Tom could not get away from his medical schooling.

Soon afterwards, we moved to a furnished one-room studio apartment across from the Medical School at Ohio State University. The place was inexpensive, and we were so glad to get out of that Allen house that it seemed close to heaven … and it was all ours! It was hard to imagine a nurse and future doctor had lived there before us, leaving behind all of that filth. Unreal! We cleaned and cleaned, then lived there for over a year. We had a kitchenette, bathroom, and livingroom/bedroom where we slept on a furnished, pull-out couch. The apartment was in a great location, so we did not need a car.

The kitchen in our apartment in Columbus, Ohio, Photographer: Thomas R. Marshall, 1955

My first big prepared meal in this apartment was inviting my whole family over for Thanksgiving dinner in 1955! Thank goodness my mom brought the turkey because I had never fixed one before. We all found a place to sit to eat, and it was a typical Thanksgiving meal. I don't know that it was very tasty, though, because I really didn't know how to cook! Mom and sister Norma did all the cooking when I lived in Mount Vernon. Tom could make several dishes well, like candied ham, rice pudding, rum cake, Spanish eggs, and many Boy Scout staple recipes which kept us alive. Smile.

My mother encouraged us kids to learn as much as we could in school so we would have more job opportunities in the future. So wherever I was living as an adult, I went to college. I started at the Mount Vernon Business College, where I think my mother took a class or two after she graduated from high school in 1926. I always kept my typing and shorthand certificate updated so I could work anywhere (well, not quite true, because a lot of prejudices existed in the Ohio work force). When I turned 21, I took a Federal Government test and got a job immediately in Columbus, Ohio, working as a secretary for the head of the department. My updated certificate kept me ready to pass this test! The first month of my marriage, after moving to Columbus, I went to college. In 1955 to 1957, I attended night school at Ohio State University, which was called "Twilight School."

I became pregnant with our first child during the fall of 1956. As I got closer to the delivery date, I moved in with Tom's mother, Daisy Dooley Marshall, in Cleveland, Ohio. She was a nurse and would know exactly what to do, in case Tom could not get away from school to be with me for the birth. Ironically, Tom was training to become an obstetrician and gynecologist!

In order to travel to my mother-in-law's house in Cleveland to prepare for the birth, I had to take my first trip alone. Instead of taking a Greyhound bus, though, I was given the wondrous opportunity to travel northward in a Pullman Sleeping Car. A Pullman was the most luxurious railroad sleeping car operated on most U.S. railroads from 1867 to 1968. I learned that African Americans were hired to serve as porters right after slavery, to capitalize on the large pool of former slaves who would be looking for work. A Pullman porter was expected to greet passengers, carry baggage, make up the sleeping berths, serve food and drinks, shine shoes, and keep the cars tidy. The porter needed to be available night and day to wait on the passengers, and he was always expected to smile, no matter how badly the customer treated him. Having a personal servant taking care of your every need was one of the biggest appeals for middle class Americans who had never had personal slaves or butlers. It was the type of treatment wealthy passengers always expected wherever they lived or traveled. Pullman porters have been widely credited with contributing to the development of the black middle class in America. My husband's sweetheart of a father, Austin Henry Marshall, happened to be a Pullman porter. He arranged this magical adventure for me. At the departure date and time, he carried the inexpensive suitcases that I received on my 18th birthday onto the train. He gallantly escorted me into my plush solo compartment. He brought me the same fine food that rich folks' ate on porcelain plates, as he smiled all the while. He even shined my shoes. Basically, he treated me like a queen, just like he would anyone who had bought an expensive ticket. It was more memorable than I can adequately describe! I so loved my father-in-law and I know he cherished me too.

Mary and Austin Marshall, 1966

We had our first child, Kathy Lynne Marshall, in May 1957, in Cleveland, under the watchful eye of nurse Daisy. During the six months that Kathy and I lived with my mother-in-law while Tom finished school, she diligently instructed me about how to care for an infant, myself, and a husband.

Once Tom graduated in 1958, we moved across country to Seattle, Washington, where he completed his medical internship, as well as fulfilled his military obligation as a Navy Lieutenant in the Medical Corps. While I nurtured 22-month old Kathy, our second child, Carrie Laureen Marshall, was born in Seattle in March 1959. Then we moved to San Diego, California, in 1961, to complete Tom's military service requirement in the Medical Corps. From 1963 to 1964, we lived in French Camp, near Stockton, California, so Tom could complete his medical residency. We actually lived in a triplex housing unit on the hospital grounds, next to the San Joaquin County Jail, where Tom fulfilled some of his medical training requirements. This location gave our family access to the cafeteria and swimming pool run by the hospital. As with most of our moves, a new baby seemed to be added to our family! We had our third child, Gregory Forrest Marshall, in French Camp in May 1963.

Someone recently asked me about my most vivid memories of being pregnant and having children. I replied, unceremoniously, "Puking!" is what I remember most. With Kathy, I was working for the Federal Government and had to go to the bathroom all the time for three months. Carrie slithered out of me so quickly that my doctor in Seattle said "Oh, you are made for having babies!" I replied, "Well, I am not going to be like my mother with seven kids!" While I was pregnant with Greg, I suspected our marriage wouldn't last much longer, so in 1962 I began taking classes at Delta College in Stockton, to prepare myself to enter the working world when the time came.

Finally, Tom was a full-fledged doctor! We moved one last time to Sacramento, California, in 1964. I made sure there would be no new baby this time!

One year later, Tom purchased a brand new house costing $16,000 in the Larchmont Riviera area in far eastern Sacramento. I still

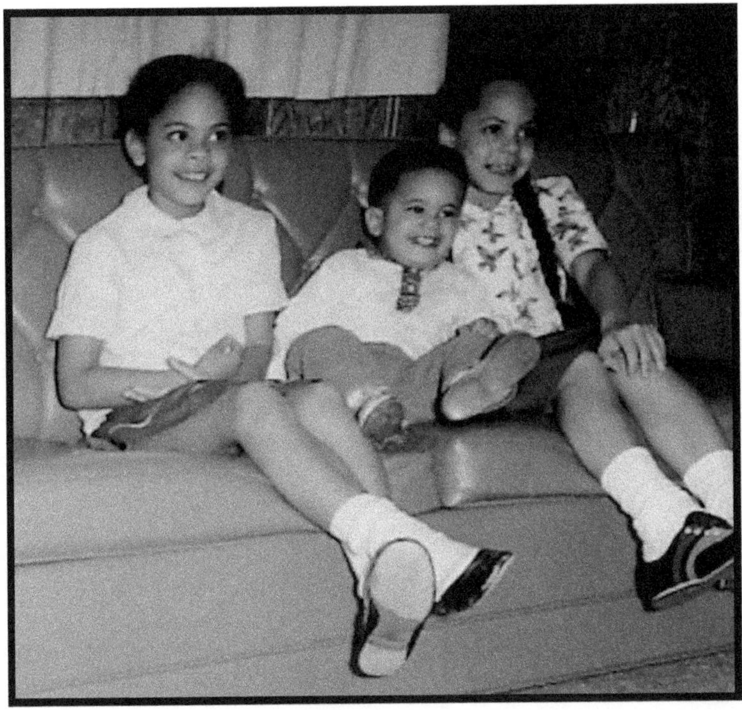

Marshall kids: Carrie, Greg, Kathy, Sacramento, CA.
Photographer: Thomas Marshall, 1965

remember the avocado green carpet and orange accents in the house! Having my own house was absolutely WONDERFUL, after spending some 30-odd years without a "pot to pee in," as my mother would say.

My husband, now Dr. Thomas R. Marshall, opened his first Obstetrics and Gynecology medical practice in South Sacramento, near the Southgate Shopping Center, where a good proportion of African Americans lived at the time. In fact, most of my friends lived in the south area, not too far from his office. I was his receptionist, assistant, and billing staff until he hired a competent woman named Myrtle to be his office manager. By then, working so closely together, and seeing each other 24 hours a day, seven days a week, our marriage was strained beyond repair.

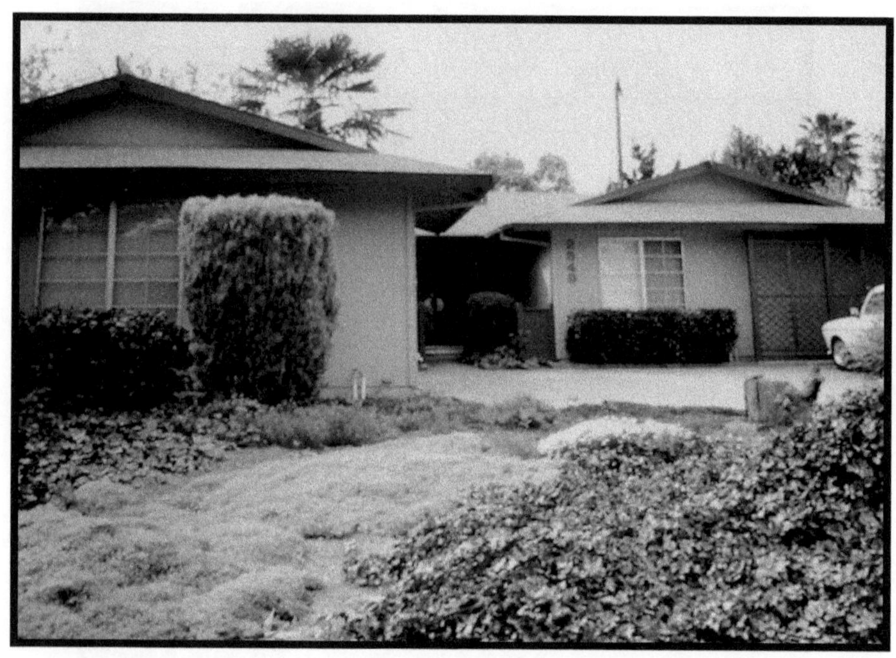

Marshall house at 2549 Key West Way, Sacramento, CA, 1979

Soon thereafter, I learned that my husband wanted a divorce in 1966 so he could marry another woman - our ballroom dance instructor that he had hired to help rekindle "our" relationship! I suspected that would happen, so I chose to continue pursuing my education. We lived on the monthly $425 that Tom had to pay in child support and alimony, until my youngest child turned 18. While the kids were at school, I was free to start going to Sacramento City College. I am proud to say that I was the first in my Carter family to earn a college degree, earning an Associate of Arts degree in 1966. Then I went on to earn a Bachelor of Arts degree in Education at Sacramento State College in 1970. I eventually earned a Masters degree in Education Administration at Sacramento State College in 1975, and even worked two-years in a Doctoral program in the 1980s but did not complete the program.

I served as an elementary school teacher for a few years and a Principal in several Sacramento City schools, including: Fairgrounds,

Freeport, Pony Express, and Bret Harte Elementary Schools. My favorite assignment was as the Principal of Camellia Basic Elementary School from 1981 to 1987. Camellia Basic School was an inner city school which was the first school in Sacramento to get a computer technology lab in 1983, stocked with Apple IIe computers.[27] It was believed computers would help jumpstart the academic progress of the 90% minority school children at Camellia who lagged behind other schools on test scores. I worked diligently as a Sacramento City Unified School District teacher and administrator for 20 years, starting at age 35 and retiring soon after my 55th birthday.

During my time as a single mother, I raised my three children on a shoestring budget. My mother taught us knitting and crocheting, but not how to cook or sew. When Kathy was born, I sewed all of her clothes, until she was six and refused to wear my poorly-made jumpsuits and dresses. Because I had little money, I gave my kids what they "needed" but not necessarily what they "wanted." I wanted them to learn to develop their own creativity and problem solving skills so they could successfully tackle any hardship. Though we were poor, we always had plenty of cheap art supplies and inexpensive fabric around the house, so they could exercise their artistic abilities and make things from scratch, including their own clothes.

One of my biggest regrets is not knowing that Kathy couldn't see. It wasn't until 5th grade that we learned Kathy needed strong glasses. On the flip side, one of my biggest pleasures was the knowledge that Carrie could skip kindergarten because she could read so well; I had always read books to my kids in an animated fashion to encourage their desire to read.

After retiring in 1989, I took Auntie Mame's[28] motto to heart: "live, Live LIVE!" I sold our family home for $160,000 more than the purchase price 30 years ago and chose to pay cash for a small, 1,100

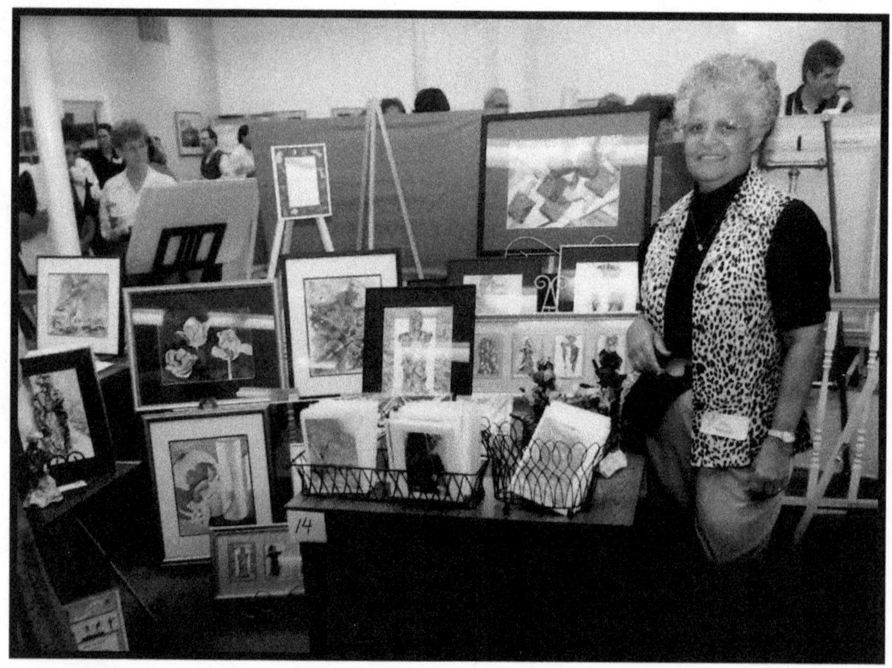

Mary Marshall at an art show selling her watercolor paintings and cards
Photographer: Kathy Marshall, 2004

square-foot home in Sun Country, an active senior complex in South Sacramento, off Stockton Boulevard and Elsie Avenue. I had only worked for 20 years and had a minimal retirement check, so I needed to ensure that I had no outstanding debts when I retired.

I had always been an artist at heart, doodling portraits on every available paper, taking draw-by-mail courses as a teenager, and using my artistic skills to dress the windows at Ringwalt's department store. As an adult, I volunteered to do various art-related activities for my Alpha Kappa Alpha sorority events, and I always added an artistic flare to my classrooms. In blessed retirement, I was free to take every art class available at Cosumnes River Community College, near my new Sun Country home. I finally focused my energies on watercolor painting. With lots of persuasion from my children, I established what ended up being a very successful "Mary Marshall Watercolors" art business. I call myself a "colorist" because I love using vivid colors in my paintings of African people, flowers, landscapes, abstracts, buildings and still life. Perhaps my most significant accomplishment was being commissioned by Antioch Baptist Progressive Church to paint a series of people from all ethnic backgrounds for the walls of their school annex.

My daughter Kathy (known as "Kanika" in the art world) and I did numerous art shows together at the Crocker Art Museum, art vendor shows, and gallery shows. I sold my watercolor paintings and Kanika would sometimes be at the vendor table next to me selling her mixed media sculptures. My daughter Carrie was, for a time, a clothing designer who used to have a business creating African-inspired clothing designs. She would sometimes be selling her wares at the table next to Kanika and me.

My son Greg had the ability to build or fix anything having to do with the house, like building a five-foot tall concrete safe for his coin collection when he was 13. He also installed a security system in my home when he was 15. He built a massive fort in the rafters of my garage and could often be found there, even in the heat of the summer, and at night. I always wondered if he had inherited those mechanical and building skills from our enslaved ancestors who we were told had mechanical skills that were utilized on their slave masters' plantations.

When I attained the wise age of 60, I became very interested in genealogy. In fact, I became almost obsessed with finding out what happened to my wayward father, who I had not seen since my fifth birthday. In the early 2000s, Kathy and I would use our personal home computers to access the Mormon's online genealogy system, or use public library computers to access Ancestry Plus (a precursor to ancestry.com). I wrote many letters to various vital information agencies in Ohio and Pennsylvania to get original birth and death certificates for my family members. I particularly wanted to know what happened to my missing father. His death certificate indicated he had died a decade earlier in 1995 in Springfield, Ohio. However, another record seemed to indicate he had died in Pennsylvania; I could never be sure which was correct. I had created several binders and writing pads full of my research, and I often collaborated with Kathy to try to make sense of it all. It was so exciting to learn about our ancestral past!

I was especially enthusiastic to learn that Ella Carter, my dad's mother, whom I called Grammie Carter, had been brought to Mount Vernon from Virginia by Columbus Delano.[29] He was Ohio's Congressional Representative and a confidant to President Lincoln. Delano helped convince Lincoln to issue the Emancipation Proclamation in 1863 to free the slaves in rebel states! My Grammie Carter took care of Delano's disabled son, and we think he rewarded her with a lovely house and beautiful furnishings as thanks for her service. We were never sure of Grammie Carter's parents and we mused that she might have actually been related to the Delanos by blood, but we have been unable to prove that assertion … yet!

I was so delighted when my girls started having children. Carrie was first, giving birth to Lauren Elise McGhee in 1981. Then Kathy had Isaac Charles Anderson in 1985 and five years later, a few days before or after my wonderful mother

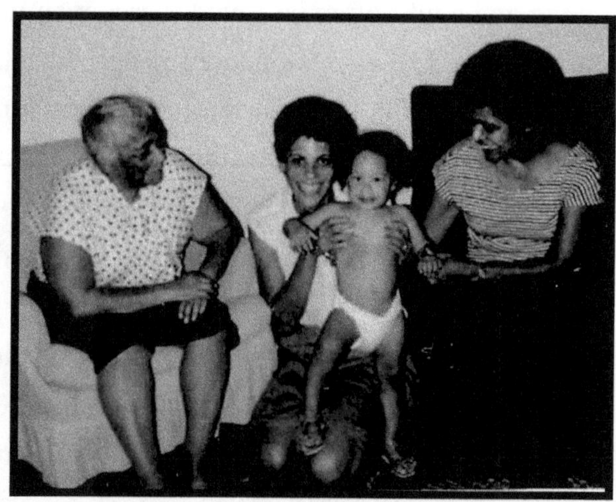

Pearl Carter, Carrie and Lauren McGhee, Mary Marshall, Columbus, Ohio, 1983

died, Matthew Thomas Anderson was conceived and born in September 1990. Son Greg has elected not to have children.

My calendar was always full with tennis tournaments, golf tournaments, sorority meetings, and bridge tournaments (I was a competitive Silver Life Master contract bridge player). We cannot forget my monthly bus trips to nearby casinos with my best friend and partner-in-crime (smile), Muriel James.

Muriel James, Mary Marshall, and Vera Pitts, bridge buddies, c. 2000

I generally tried to keep Saturdays and Sundays free, though, so my kids and grandkids could drop by for a visit. I felt blessed that they chose to spend their free time with me. I enjoyed all of them thoroughly, especially when the grandkids would spend the night in my enclosed sunroom that lead to my petite backyard! It was fun trying to teach them to play golf at nearby 9–hole golf courses, and tennis at the tennis courts in my active adult community. My grandkids had the potential to be very good players and I voiced on several occasions that it would make me so happy if they tried out for the high school tennis or golf team. But, alas, they never did. None of my kids or grandkids chose to play bridge or do any sports that Tom and I did. Perhaps they had no inclination to do so because Tom and I are too competitive!

Lauren was always to sweet and helpful, like my sister Betty. Isaac and Matthew became excellent at taekwondo and Matthew played the quints[30] drums in the Franklin High School symphonic and marching band, and their award-winning drumline. I still cannot imagine how he could have five different-sized drums around his waist

(L to R:) Matthew and Ken Anderson, Romeo and Carrie Malenab, Lauren McGhee, Mary Marshall, Isaac Anderson, Photographer: Kathy Marshall, Elk Grove, CA, 1991

and seemingly play them all at the same time, while walking in formation with the rest of the band. He certainly did not get his rhythm or musical skills from me!

In 1996, when I was just 62 years old, I found a lump in my left breast. I had breast cancer. Me? I was always more physically active than any female I knew. I did not smoke or drink and I ate healthy meals (except for a little See's Candies chocolate bridge mix, or chocolate turtles every now and then). I played competitive tennis and golf, rode my bicycle often, and regularly went to the gym. As far as I knew, except for maybe one of my aunts who was always very private about her business, there was no incidence of breast cancer in my family. Prior to my generation, we were a very long-lived people, with most of our elderly family members living into their 90s. But I got breast cancer, the doctors later mused that perhaps I had taken estrogen hormone replacement therapy for too long a period back in the 1960s and 1970s. Never one to shy away from doing what needs to be done, I scheduled mastectomy surgery right away.

It was excruciatingly important to me that my girls knew how to do breast self-examinations. They would learn from me what a cancerous lump felt like so they would be sure to catch any cancers that they might have early. After the surgery, the scar from my removed left breast, and the itchy radiation burns from my combined chemotherapy and radiation, had to be endured for the rest of my life.

I was devoid of cancer for seven years, but it came back... aggressively metastasizing, eventually into my brain. I bravely fought the disease off and on for three more years, being extremely ill every summer and feeling a little better during the winters. During those last months of 2006, Kathy and I worked to complete a journal of stories about my life, entitled "*Reflections from a Mother's Heart.*" The book was given to me by my good friend Patsy Haynes nine years prior, but I had not finished writing in it. I am grateful that Kathy has chosen to populate this book with many of my memories so my grandkids and their future children can know me through my life stories.

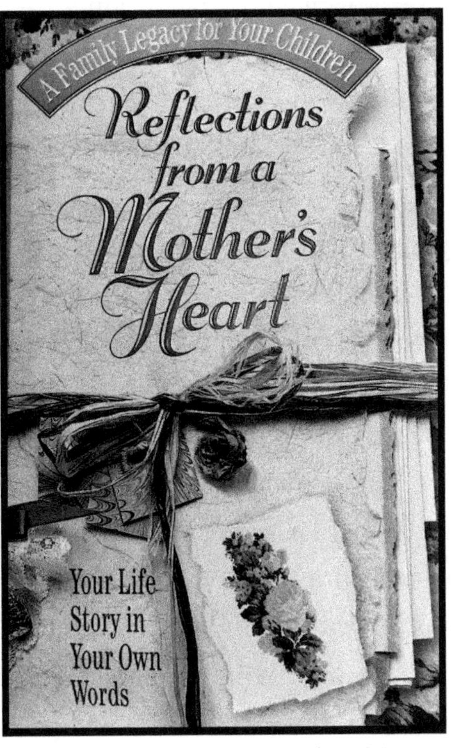

Mary Marshall's Journal, 2006

I was born on Easter Sunday and named Mary, after Jesus' mother. I have always felt that God had a special place in my life, a special calling every day! I am not a churchgoer because I have not had really good experiences in churches. I feel they are too man-made. However, as I look back on my life, there was always a special guidance, a spiritual feeling, that helped me live a very good, clean life. I have always felt that living a productive life of service and fun was the way to go. I feel too many people do not take advantage of being alive each day! They allow too many negatives to color their perceptions, and cause strife and drama when it does not need to exist.

Mary Marshall's "Doorway to Myself," Sacramento, California, October 2006

I feel that God answered my prayers when my son Greg began taking (and later carrying) me to the Spiritual Life Center in August 2006, after I learned I only had six months to live. That church gave me such solace during my last months on Earth, especially their Reverend Dr. Francione who personally talked with me about the afterlife. They shared my belief of Many Paths to the One God. I think religion should be inclusive, not discriminatory against any group or any belief. I do not support so-called religious people who proselytize their own brand of religion at the expense of others. There are Many Paths to God and each is acceptable, in my opinion. I am now at peace.

My spiritual legacy to my family and friends was the last painting I created after my final diagnosis, called "Doorway to Myself." It is like nothing I have ever previously painted. I felt as though my hand was guided by a spiritual force to paint this image of a doorway where the doors don't quite close. Having been claustrophobic all my life from the very tight quarters we had growing up, I wanted my afterlife to be open, so I could pass through whenever I wanted.

What one word best describes my life? FORTUNATE! Being at the right place at the right time: growing up, education, career, and retirement. My children and family have been my most treasured possessions. I shall miss them all terribly. The only dream that may not be fulfilled is making it to the age of 80…

[Author's Notes: My mother Mary Ellen Marshall was born in 1934, 100 years after our enslaved ancestor, Otho Williams, was born. She joined the ancestors on January 27, 2007, from her bed in Sacramento, California, at the age of 72. Now mom is with her parents, siblings, grandparents and her formerly enslaved ancestors. I believe all of our ancestors continue to look out for us - their living descendants - from on high.

My mother lived the life she wanted to live, blessing others with her positive spirit, organizational skills, creativity, athleticism and boundless energy. Mom showed her children, grandchildren, friends, family and the school kids she mentored, how to be good citizens and to serve our community well.

Like my dad, mom was a compartmentalized individual who had a lot of interests. Her life was like a pie chart, with equal slices representing her love of her immediate and remote family, her many and varied friends, her art business, her Alpha Kappa Alpha sorority, her love of competitive sports her competitive contract bridge tournaments, and her job.

She was a great planner and organizer and she lived within her means (even with occasional trips to the casino!). I could not have had a better role model for a mother, artist, or career woman! Mom was, and will always be, my hero!

The thoughts presented in "The Principal Artist" were derived from census, marriage, and divorce records, as well as documented interviews with Mary's cousin, Lavata Williams, and her brother, Dale Carter, children Carrie Malenab and Greg Marshall. The entries from Mary Marshall's personal journal were heavily represented in this chapter, along with the author's first-hand knowledge of her mother.]

The ancestors are smiling!

Chapter 9: The Doctor Athlete

From the Mouth of Dr. Thomas Richard Marshall

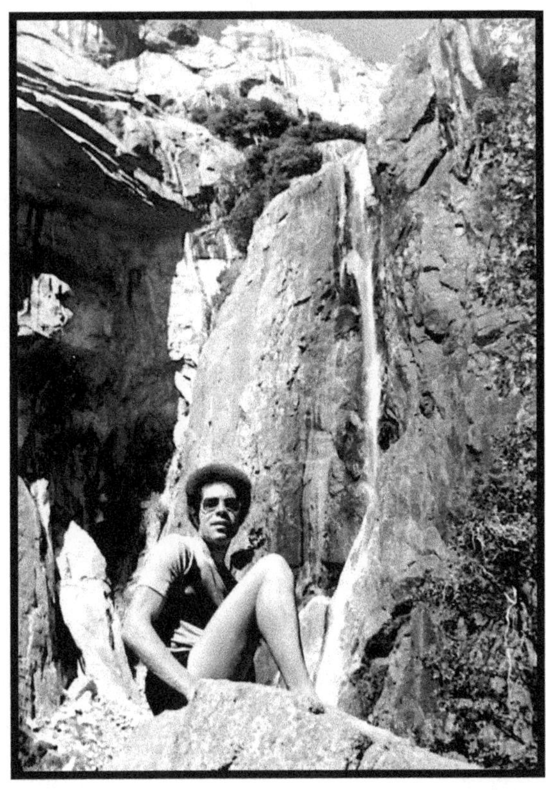

> *"I met Thomas Marshall when I was 18 years old, in 1952. He drove to Mount Vernon, Ohio, with a friend from Cleveland, to pick up my sister, Sara, at my house to go skating in Zanesville. There was space in the car so I went along, since I enjoy skating too. Tom was funny – very much unlike boys from Mount Vernon. He was in college and was planning to go to medical school. He was 21. He was tall (I like tall men!) He was articulate and could carry on a conversation, and he really wanted to see me again! The meeting was very good – Fun, relaxing, and very enjoyable!"*
>
> *- Mary Ellen Marshall, "Reflections from a Mother's Heart"*

The first thing you must know about me, Dr. Thomas Richard Marshall, is that I love sunsets. Wherever I have traveled throughout the world - and I have visited many countries - I bring back scores of incredible photographs of my beloved sunsets. I believe a beautiful sunset is a visually spectacular way to end a day that otherwise may have seemed to be an ordinary one.

The next thing that you must know is that I love to run long distances … fast, fast enough to beat you! My favorite activity while running any long-distance race is to catch up to the runner ahead of me, make a little small talk, smile casually, then lengthen my long-legged stride, passing them in the dust like they are standing still! I have lean muscular legs, incredible lung capacity and the motivation to win. I am a running enthusiast who, some have said, runs like a gazelle. A member of the Buffalo Chips Running Club in Sacramento, California, I have several times run the 26.2-mile Boston Marathon, Courtland Twenty Miler along the River Road south of Sacramento, the California International Marathon, and several other marathons around the world. Usually, I earn qualifying times and sometimes win awards for my age group.

My mother says I could have been born a duck, because I love all water sports. Learning to swim at the Cleveland YMCA on Cedar Avenue in the late 1940s, I soon became a lifeguard and competitive swimmer. Later in life, I was the captain of my own sailboat and a kayaker in numerous mini-triathlon competitions which consist of running, swimming and bicycling.

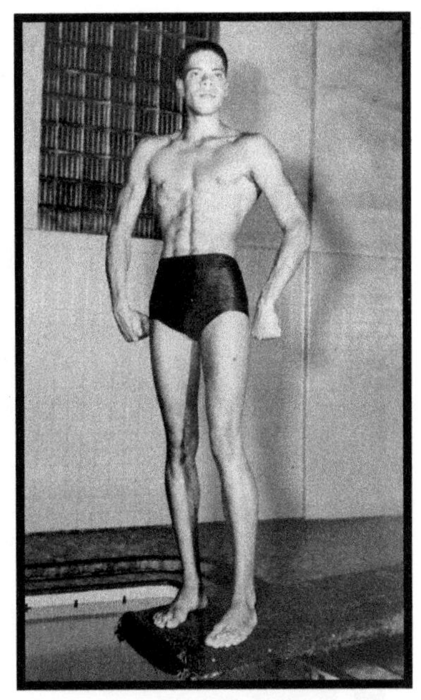

Thomas Marshall, lifeguard at YMCA, Cleveland, 1949

It is hard to know whether I like bicycling, running, or swimming the best. Since 1946, when I got my first bicycle license, I have entered and sometimes won many long-distance bicycling competitions, including the Tahoe Sierra Century 100-miler race in Lake Tahoe, California.

I did have one formidable mishap when I was in my 50s, though. A spare tire got caught in my bicycle spokes as I was coming down a particularly steep hill in Yosemite, California. This resulted in a head-over-bike crash. Doctors feared I would never walk again, as my left ankle was shattered, yet my indomitable spirit spurred me on to continue entering triathlon competitions into my 70s!

But I am most proud to claim that I am an award-winning Iron Man.[31] Perhaps the ultimate test of human endurance and drive is for one person to complete an Iron Man Triathlon, which generally consists of a 26.2 mile marathon, two-mile swim in open water, and 100-mile bicycle trip, all in one day. I have done that several times in Hawaii and Mexico. To me, the Iron Man Triathlon is the height of endurance training and I am proud to have proven that I am a bonafide Iron Man!

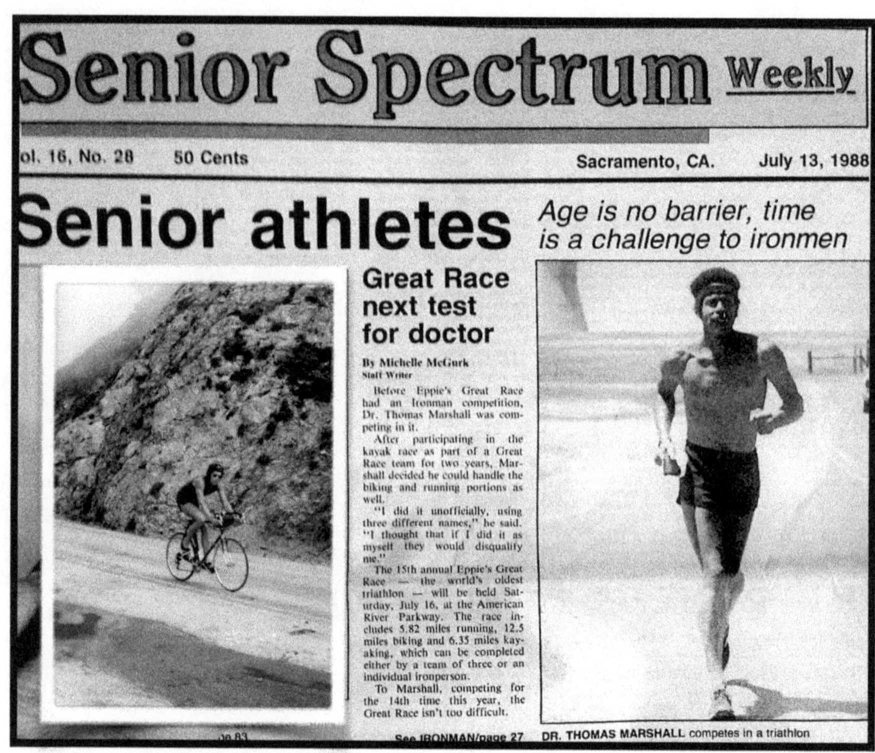

Senior Spectrum Weekly

ol. 16, No. 28 50 Cents Sacramento, CA. July 13, 1988

Senior athletes

Age is no barrier, time is a challenge to ironmen

Great Race next test for doctor

By Michelle McGurk
Staff Writer

Before Eppie's Great Race had an Ironman competition, Dr. Thomas Marshall was competing in it.

After participating in the kayak race as part of a Great Race team for two years, Marshall decided he could handle the biking and running portions as well.

"I did it unofficially, using three different names," he said. "I thought that if I did it as myself they would disqualify me."

The 15th annual Eppie's Great Race — the world's oldest triathlon — will be held Saturday, July 16, at the American River Parkway. The race includes 5.82 miles running, 12.5 miles biking and 6.35 miles kayaking, which can be completed either by a team of three or an individual ironperson.

To Marshall, competing for the 14th time this year, the Great Race isn't too difficult.

See IRONMAN/page 27

DR. THOMAS MARSHALL competes in a triathlon

Thomas Marshall Competing in "Eppie's Great Race" in a mini-Triathlon in Sacramento, California, Age 57, Source: Senior Spectrum, 1988

For 25 years in a row, I did Eppie's Great Race, known as the "The World's Oldest Triathlon" which was started in Sacramento, California. Although this race was only 5.8 miles running, 12.5 miles biking, and 6.35 miles kayaking down the American River, I was the first one - albeit unofficially - to do all of the events all by myself in the mid-1970s, instead of in teams of three athletes, like everybody else. My unpredictable medical schedule made it impossible to work in a team. This "do-it-all-yourself" style of competing later became known as the Iron Man Triathlon. I claim the title as the first Iron Man! In 1999, in "*Eppie's Great Race: How It All Began,*" they acknowledged that "Dr. Thomas Marshall completed his 25th straight race, missing only the inaugural event because he didn't know about it."[32]

As you can tell, I think pretty highly of myself and my abilities. I have never felt less than any man or woman, whether they be white or black. You may ask how a black man in racially-charged America could be so sure of himself? Really, it was all due to my parents and where we lived during my formative years.

I was born in 1931, at the start of the Great Depression. I was fortunate to grow up in the metropolitan city of Cleveland, Ohio. Throughout most of the 19th century, the social and economic status of Afro-Americans[33] in Cleveland was superior to that in other northern communities. Segregation was infrequent in the mid-1800s and interracial violence rarely occurred there. Almost one-third of Afro-Americans were skilled workers and some had accumulated wealth. However, after the Great Migration,[34] the increase in black population caused racism to rear its ugly head. In the early 1900s, fewer Afro-Americans were allowed to participate in foundries and steel mills, and blacks were starting to be excluded from some restaurants and housing.

However, the Depression's New Deal relief programs helped to reduce black unemployment, even though segregation in housing continued. Businesses in black neighborhoods began to thrive during the period from the 1920s to the 1940s. It was one of political change, with the balance of support in Cleveland moving toward the Democratic Party.

As a result, discrimination and segregation was ended at City Hospital, which opened up medicine as an achievable career choice for me and other blacks. Afro-Americans finally had the chance to be fully educated and became skilled in the professions, and I would become one of them!

My daddy, Austin Henry Marshall, was a Pullman porter by the 1920s, servicing the every need and whim of white patrons on the luxurious Pullman train cars. His train route started in the deep south of

Columbus, Georgia, where he was born in 1892 to Henry Marshall and Mary Smith Marshall. Then his train route went northwest to St. Louis, Missouri, where he met my mother, then north to Columbus, Ohio.

Austin Henry Marshall, Cleveland, Ohio, Photographer: Thomas R. Marshall, 1953

Daddy also proudly served in World War I as a Private first class, in Meuse-Argonne, France, as part of the American Expeditionary Forces, from 1918 to 1919. He was treated so well in France, like an equal human being, and he was honorably discharged in March 1919. Coming back to America, though, he was once again beset with pervasive racism everywhere.

For all of my growing years until I was an adult, my daddy was home only a few days each month and worked on the train the rest of the time. It was grueling and often demeaning work, but Pullman porters could make good money from tips, compared to most Afro-American men at the time, and they were respected in the black community. Daddy always dressed well, whether he was in his uniform or walking around town between train trips. He was always in my corner and believed in me, no matter what his friends said about me. Ultimately, my dad was integral in making me into the man-doctor I eventually became.

Daddy's difficult work schedule left my mother, Daisy Rae Dooley Marshall, as the practical and capable head of our household.

Mother was born in Noxubee County, Mississippi, in 1902, to William Dooley and Julia Nicholson. Her family had moved to St. Louis, Missouri, by 1910, and that is where my parents likely met, since St. Louis was on daddy's train route. In 1921, they married and moved to Cleveland, Ohio.

Daisy Dooley Marshall, Cleveland, Ohio, 1940

Mother was a very well-respected woman in the Afro-American community. She was an alumnus of the Western Reserve School of Mortuary Science, as well as graduate from the Frances P. Bolton School of Practical Nursing. Mother was allegedly the first black woman in Ohio to be an Associate Funeral Home Director and embalmer. Mother and one of my dad's brothers managed the Marshall Funeral Home in Cleveland, from 1939 to 1950.

Yes, believe it or not, my two sisters, two brothers and I grew up in the Marshall Funeral Home, with our family living upstairs and the funeral "preparation room" being in the basement. In some odd way, perhaps this proximity to death helped me become interested in becoming a medical doctor to *save* peoples' lives. Oh the funny stories I could tell you about growing up in a funeral home! Like the day my smart-aleck mouth angered my petite dynamo of a Mortician mother so much that she ran up the stairs from the basement after me … with a cleaver in her tiny, feminine hand; don't ask me what she was doing with a cleaver in the basement...

After the Funeral Home closed in 1950, my family moved to a three-story shotgun house[35] on East Boulevard in Cleveland, and that is when mother became a licensed practical nurse who worked for

Marshall Funeral Home, Cleveland, Ohio, left to right: Thomas, Austin Jr., Shirley Jean, Patricia, c. 1940

Lakeside Hospital until she retired in 1967. Mother lived the last years of her life in a University Hospital from about 1980 to 1986, after Alzheimer's took her marvelous brain. For over 50 years, mother had been an active member of the St. James A.M.E. church and was a precinct committee member for the Democratic Party and American League. She was a tough, very-driven, no-nonsense woman, but I worshipped her and have always been thankful she was my mother.

Needless to say, my strong and active parents greatly influenced the lives and career choices of us Marshall kids. We were all expected to succeed in life.

My sister, Patricia Rae Marshall (1926-2010), was the oldest child who was often left in charge of us "knuckleheads" as she affectionately called us. Patricia became a concert pianist and Professor at the Cleveland Institute of Music. She had three husbands and five children: Jocelyn, Scott, Marsha, Francina, and Kevin Connors. Pat and

I spent many vacations together as we grew older and we always kept in close contact.

My older brother, Austin Henry Marshall Jr. (1929-1979), became a postal carrier in Cleveland. He and his wife, Bernadine, had two children: Pershell and Austin David who, if I may say, looks a lot like the younger me! Austin and his wife spent some time with me in California, with my brother trying to recuperate from an aneurism before he passed away.

My younger sister, Shirley Jean (1935-1971) was very social and loved the street life. She was really a lot of fun and we loved to play cards. Jean's three children - Michal, Carolyn and Lori - had to be raised by my mother, who gave them a very strong work ethic which helped them all to grow into productive citizens.

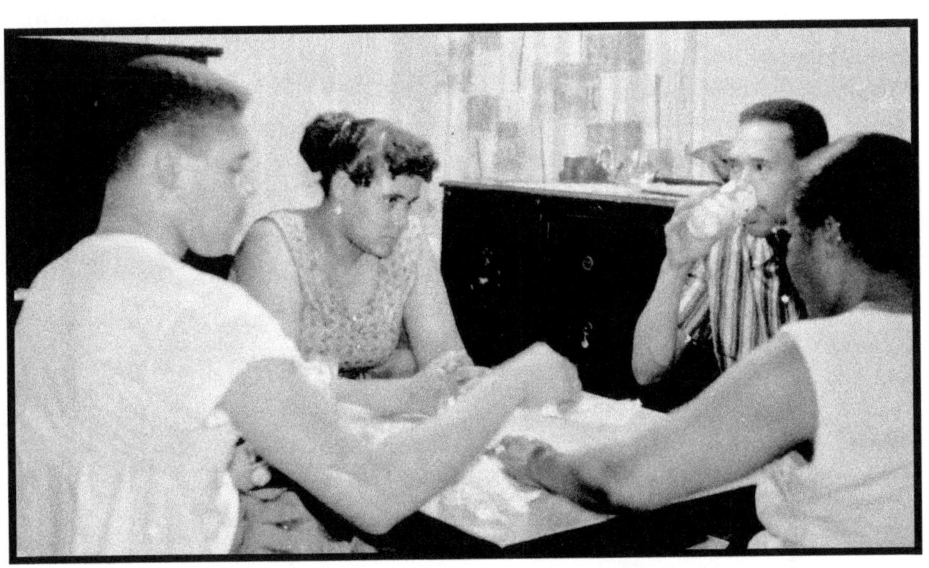

Thomas, Jean, Austin and Patricia playing cards, Cleveland, Ohio, c. 1952

My youngest sibling, Bruce Cyril Marshall (1940-2017?) was an entrepreneur all of his life. He moved his gorgeous wife, Rae Evelyn Gardner (1944-2010), and their four sons, Bruce, Terrell, Jason, and

Christopher Marshall, to Sacramento, California, in 1968. They became the closest family, in proximity, that my children had throughout their formative years.

As the middle child, I went to East Tech High School in my hometown of Cleveland, graduating in 1949 with an emphasis in chemistry and higher mathematics. Mother was always very proud of me - even with my occasional high-spirited antics. She often called me "doctor" when I was a child, instead of Thomas, hoping to instill in me the desire to become a medical professional like herself… and it worked!

I attended Case Western Reserve University from 1949 to 1953, following a Pre-Med curriculum. By then, our country was fighting in the Korean War. I received a deferral because of my schooling; but every year, I had to supply the Selective Service with my academic record or be drafted into the military!

Cut along this line to detach card

SELECTIVE SERVICE SYSTEM
NOTICE OF CLASSIFICATION

Approval of Budget Bureau not required

Marshall (Last name) Thomas (First name) R. (Middle name)

Selective Service No. 33 | 22 | 31 | 132

has been classified in Class 1-A (Until ...., 19......) by ☒ Local Board. ☐ Appeal Board, by vote of .... to .... ☐ President (Show vote on appeal board cases only)

Feb. 28, 1951 (Date of mailing) (Member of local board)

(Registrant must sign here)

The law requires you, subject to heavy penalty for violation, to carry this notice, in addition to your Registration Certificate, on your person at all times—to exhibit it upon request to authorized officials—to surrender it, upon entering the armed forces, to your commanding officer.

For advice, see your Government appeal agent.

The law requires you: (1) To keep in touch with your local board; (2) to notify it of any change of address; (3) to notify it of any fact which might change your classification; (4) to comply with the instructions on the notice of classification part of this form.

SSS Form No. 110 (Revised 4-15-49)

Cut along this line to detach card

16—81524-6 U. S. GOVERNMENT PRINTING OFFICE

Thomas Marshall's Selective Service Certification, 1951

The next five years were grueling, exciting, fun, tiring, and educational. The Ohio State University of Medicine was supposed to be my primary focus from 1953 to 1958. It was nationally recognized as a top institution in both education and research, and was chosen to be among the 21 hospitals named to U.S. News and World Report's select honor roll of U.S. Hospitals. My school fees were generally $165 per semester, paid by my supportive Pullman porter daddy, and the rest of my living expenses were supplemented by my part-time job as a chauffeur.

During this time, I met the lovely Mary Ellen Carter, kind of on a blind date when I met her through her sister Sara. We went to a skating rink 2.5 hours away from me, in Zanesville, Ohio. I could not get her out of my mind after we skated together. Our letters to each other increased, as did our passion. She was living in the small town of Mount Vernon, which was about one hour's drive from Ohio State University. I was delighted when she agreed to be my wife! After she turned 21, we married in 1955, and moved into a tiny apartment near my school.

Thomas Marshall and Mary Carter, Columbus, 1953

I was deeply in love and sometimes my studies suffered. In fact, my daddy received warning notices from the school indicating that I might fail medical school. His friends told him that I was a no-good, goof-off and he should stop wasting his hard-earned money on my education.

My dear son:
How are you? Fine I hope. I see that you are not making your marks, I got a letter today, it seem that you won't be there long, unless you change and get your lessons, and if you don't they are going to let you out, then the Army is going to get you. Then what are you going to do?

You talking about Mary coming to Columbus, it seems that you are not going to be there long. I was told before I sent you there, that I was throwing away money, I hope it not true. If they send you to the Army, what will you do about Mary then? You better think about yourself and get your lessons. Here is the report, so suit yourself.

Daddy

PS. They told me to send this to you.

Letter from Austin Marshall to his son Thomas who was failing Medical School, 1954

When daddy wrote me a poignant letter pouring out his disappointment in me, I finally realized just how much faith he actually had in me, even though others did not. I soon righted my ship and began to study avidly. During this time, my first child, Kathy Lynne Marshall, was born in Cleveland in 1957, under the watchful eye of my mother, then-nurse Daisy.

With the urging and support of my family, I graduated from medical school in 1958.

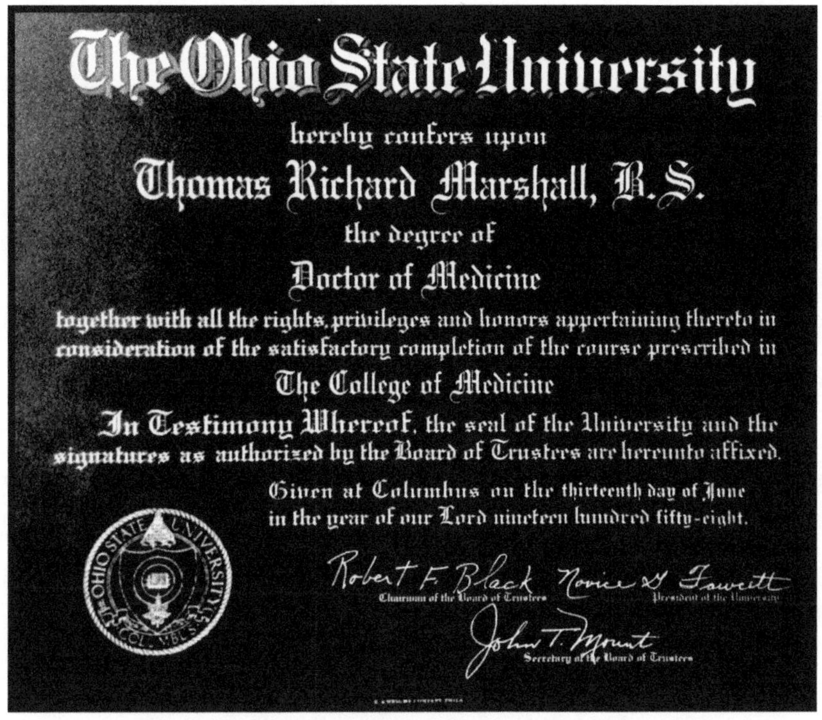

The Ohio State University

hereby confers upon

Thomas Richard Marshall, B.S.

the degree of

Doctor of Medicine

together with all the rights, privileges and honors appertaining thereto in consideration of the satisfactory completion of the course prescribed in

The College of Medicine

In Testimony Whereof, the seal of the University and the signatures as authorized by the Board of Trustees are hereunto affixed.

Given at Columbus on the thirteenth day of June in the year of our Lord nineteen hundred fifty-eight.

Doctor of Medicine from The Ohio State University for Thomas Richard Marshall, 1958

From graduation until 1961, my family was sent to Seattle, Washington, so I could serve my military obligation as a Lieutenant in the Medical Corps of the Navy Reserves. Seattle is also where my second child, Carrie Laureen Marshall, was born. There, I finished my medical internship. I was also introduced to sailing, which became a life-long passion. I must admit that I had such a great time in Seattle, kayaking and hiking in

Thomas loved sailing, San Diego, c. 1962

Olympic National Park, boating and swimming, and camping. It was a Boy Scout's dream come true!

The military then sent me to Camp Pendleton in San Diego from 1961 to 1962, where I again served as a Lieutenant in the Medical Corps. Of course, work was only a necessary requirement, whereas sailing and scuba diving and my family were my loves.

From 1963 to 1964, I finished my medical residency in Stockton and French Camp, California. That is where my son, Gregory Forrest Marshall, was born. I worked as a medic in the County Jail and at the San Joaquin County Hospital. Conveniently, my family lived in a triplex with other doctors' families on the hospital grounds.

Finally, I was ready to open my first Obstetric-Gynecology medical practice in 1965, in a one-story medical building on Florin Road and Franklin Boulevard, in South Sacramento. I delivered babies and performed surgeries at Methodist and Sutter Memorial Hospitals.

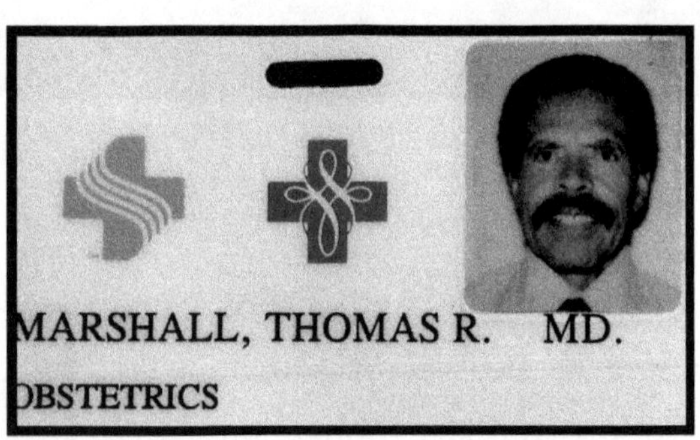

Dr. Thomas R. Marshall, 1965 - 2001

One of the most memorable moments in my entire life was when my daddy and his second wife, Vernelle, visited my first medical office in 1966, a year before he died. His joy at my medical achievements gave me more humble pleasure than I can describe! His friends were wrong; his money was not wasted on me!

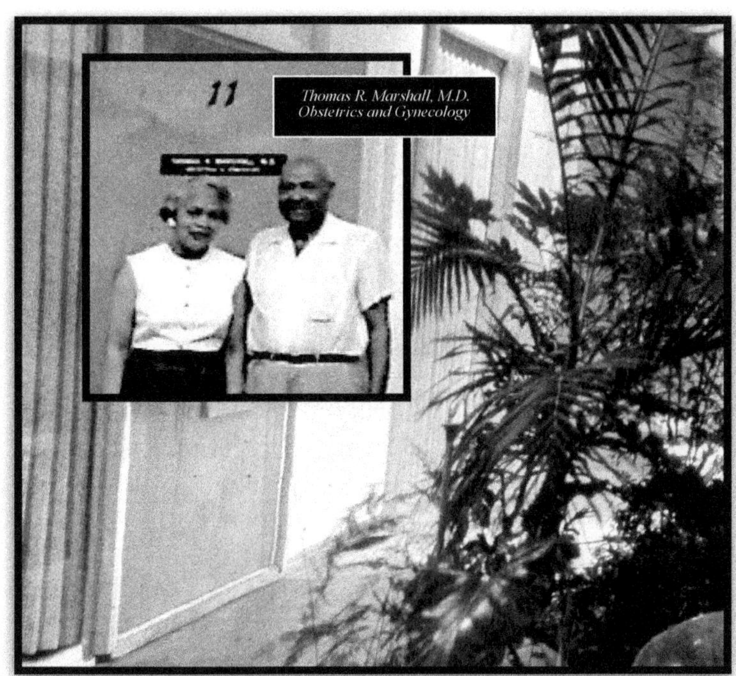

Vernelle and Austin Marshall at son Dr. Thomas Marshall's Office
Southgate Medical Center, Sacramento, California, 1966

A Tiny Sample of the Babies Delivered by Dr. Thomas R. Marshall,
Photographer: Jennifer Briones, 2013

Over the years, I moved my medical practice to a larger building located at Freeport and Florin Road. My last medical office was on Coyle Avenue in Carmichael, California, where I was also working at Mercy-San Juan Hospital during my last 15 or so years of practicing medicine. I don't know for sure, but I estimate I helped bring well over 1,000 babies into the world, and helped many more women with various genealogical health and surgical issues over my 35-year professional medical career. On several occasions, I also gladly took the opportunity to participate in "Doctors Without Borders" providing humanitarian medical aid in Mexico and the Philippines.

In 1965, when arriving in Sacramento, I moved my family to an all-white neighborhood in the suburbs far-east of Sacramento, CA. I purchased my first brand-new house for $16,000. Nobody was going to tell me where I could and could not live!

After a hard day's work, I loved more than anything else telling stories to my kids' neighborhood friends. We would gather into my study, which was our third bedroom where I stored all of my office and personal belongings. I would close the door and curtains to darken the room, then would proceed to tell them scary stories that I learned when I was a Boy Scout in Cleveland. My favorite was Edgar Allen Poe's "Tell Tale Heart" which I recited with dramatic perfection:

> *...You fancy me mad. Madmen know nothing. But you should have seen me. You should have seen how wisely I proceeded — with what caution — with what foresight — with what dissimulation I went to work! I was never kinder to the old man than during the whole week before I killed him...*[36]

Then suddenly, I would grab the closest child by the arm! Squeals of fear and delight abounded! For some reason, I loved scaring the children until they screamed! If I may say so, I was a good doctor who could have been a phenomenal actor.

As charming and funny as I could be to friends, colleagues, and patients, I couldn't be expected to be at the peak of performance all the time, could I? At home, I could let out my stresses a bit, couldn't I? Well, my wife didn't think so. She did not like being demeaned by me or yelled at, or treated to the other ways in which I chose to de-stress. Our marriage was becoming more tense with each new city-move of our family. I thought that if Mary and I learned to dance together, then we would become close again, so I enrolled us in Ballroom Dance classes at Salazar's Dance Studio on Auburn Blvd. Our teacher was a ravishing beauty named Pamala Swift. When you think of a raven-haired tango dancer in a shockingly-red dress, with flawless white-powdered skin and vibrant kissable lips, you will understand that I was immediately smitten with our teacher! I soon started taking solo dance lessons with her. It did not take long for me to be thoroughly under Pam's spell and in 1966, I divorced Mary so I could marry Pam. Pam and I lived together in her small apartment off Fulton Avenue while I had the renowned Sacramento architect, Carter Sparks,[37] build us a magnificent tri-level, avant-garde Executive Home. It would be built into the side of a hilltop on a 28-acre lot in the foothills. In the late 1960s, Loomis and Rocklin, California, were very rural areas with peach orchards and granite quarries, about 30 minutes east of Sacramento. I had a huge lake dug out in the lower level of the property. The lake was fed by a small stream and inhabited by large-mouth bass. Pam had an innate sense of design drama and she outfitted our home with long black and purple shag carpet, along with a red-pink-purple-orange striped velvety sofa in

Pamala Swift, c. 1967

the sunken livingroom in the bottom level. I required the builders to use locally-sourced granite rock inside the house for the lower-level fireplace, as well as surrounding the supportive walls of the spiral staircase. The floors were made from black slate. Rustic wood was on all walls, interior and exterior. I absolutely loved this property and ended up living there for 30 years.

Marshall House in Loomis, California, Photographer: Kathy Marshall, 2000

My kids came to visit us every other weekend, and two weeks during the summer while they were young. I always gave them chores to complete while I was away at the hospital, like using buckets to gather water from the lake and hand-watering the trees I planted around the property. The kids were also asked to dig out rocks from the naturally rocky soil, and help me build rock retaining walls around the property, using those dug-up stones. We even had goats to help mow down the grasses and weeds on the hillside. It was a magnificent home!

At night, we swam under the majestic stars in my 50-foot long oval pool, after a delicious BBQ dinner often cooked by me, followed by my mother's special bread pudding or my dad's signature rum cake. My kids also came over for birthdays and our annual Christmas Eve celebration, opening gifts under my stately 14' Christmas tree, whose lights were reflected prettily in my floor-to-ceiling glass wall windows.

Unfortunately, my second marriage ended in only four years. Pam accused me of being too "difficult." Her lawyer arranged for her to take more than half of my property, but I kept my dream house and 14 acres. Even after our divorce, my very kind mother-in-law, Emma Swift, would still visit me and my kids periodically from Michigan, where she lived. I wasn't all bad. In fact, I am actually a very sentimental guy, but my behavior at home can sometimes be a problem.

Over the next several years, I had several female companions, but most came and went, except for one long-term relationship in the 1980s. Of course, I never felt those relationship failures were my fault. Those women just couldn't understand how stressful it was to have to be kind, patient and knowledgeable all the time. A doctor's only respite is unwinding at home, right? Well, none of those ladies understood, until 1988, when I met a beautiful blond named

Virginia Harbridge and Thomas Marshall, wedding, Sacramento, California, 1994

Virginia Harbridge during a medical encounter.

Virginia and I began dating and we quickly fell in love. I had never been with a woman whom I felt literally worshipped at my feet. I loved her loving attention! She was so kind and gentle. We began living together in the Loomis house. Slowly, the bohemian elements of Pam's 1970's home design esthetic began to disappear from the house, being replaced with white leather sofas and chairs. White china replaced Pam's heavy, rustic stoneware plates. Rustic was slowly replaced with a more streamlined, refined esthetic.

In 1992, we had Carter Sparks design a vacation house for us in Shelter Cove, which is a small fishing village on the "Lost Coast" of California, a 5.5 hour drive northwest from Sacramento. Virginia and I would drive up on weekends to relax at our vacation home. It was marvelous looking at the ocean from our balcony … until someone

Second Marshall home in Shelter Cove, California
Photographer: Kathy Marshall, c. 2006

dared to build a house across the street, right in front of our ocean view! After we married in 1994, we decided to have another house built in Shelter Cove, but this time it would be right at the edge of a cliff, overlooking the wide expanse of the Pacific Ocean. This was on a lot that geologists had previously determined was geologically unstable. But build we did, and it was more magnificent than the first home, which we later sold.

Like all of my houses, this third home was a Carter Sparks original, using locally sourced rock and wood to enhance the natural surroundings. When I retired from my medical practice, we moved permanently to Shelter Cove in 2002. I loved building the detached garage with my son, Greg, and wife, Virginia. I could be found endlessly tinkering with the sprinkler systems and building wire fences to keep the deer out of our yard. Our favorite perch was in the backyard, partially down the hillside, looking directly onto the Pacific Ocean. We installed a metal bench there and, with a glass of wine, would ruminate on nothing but the setting sun and the sparkling ocean. There is no prettier place to watch a sunset than in my own backyard!

Around the time I retired at the age of 70, in 2001, I was having a hard time finding the right words to convey my thoughts. Do you know what I mean? The word you are searching for is right at the tip of your tongue, but you can't quite access it? Something was going on inside my brain that I could not identify and I couldn't stop. After many tests, the doctors first said I had Alzheimer's Disease, like my mother. Later, they changed the diagnosis to frontal lobe dementia. This is a condition which would slowly continue to eat away at my brain control centers, like speech, then mobility. Eventually, we had to move back to the Sacramento area in 2009 for medical care. Even though my brain was functioning, I could not speak or walk by myself.

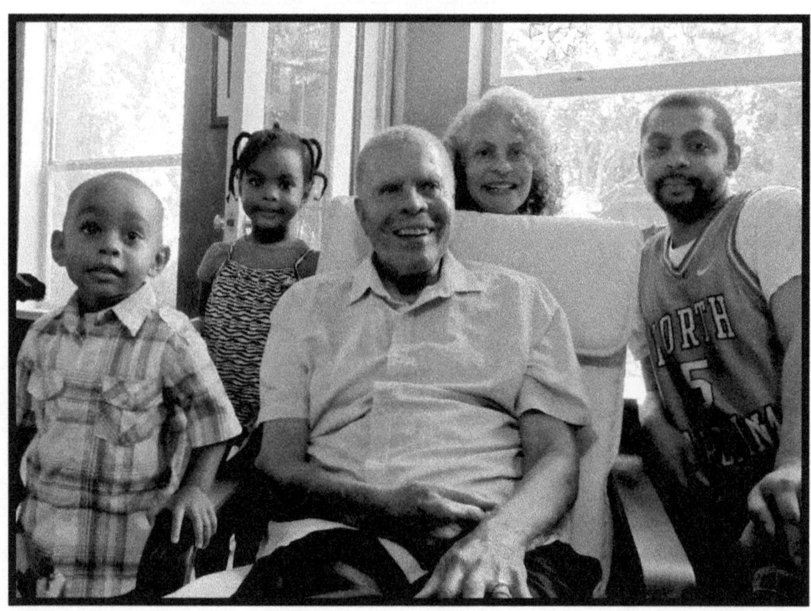

Isaiah and Jazmine Anderson, Thomas and Kathy Marshall, Isaac Anderson,Carmichael, CA, Photographer: Virginia Marshall, 2013

Thankfully, I could still enjoy the constant, loving attention from my devoted wife, and visits from friends, my kids, grandkids, and great grandkids. I particularly enjoyed when children came over, so I could watch them play and laugh with delight. Often, we would go to the neighborhood park, with the kids playing and me watching them contentedly. The kids would be gentle and respectful, and not too loud around me.

Thomas Marshall, middle, Cleveland, Ohio, 1947

Looking back on my life, I realize that I did everything I wanted to do. I played the trumpet in junior and senior high school, and bought my first flute while I was in medical school. I bought my first professional Nikon camera while a resident in Stockton, so I could take pictures of my sunsets wherever and whenever I wished.

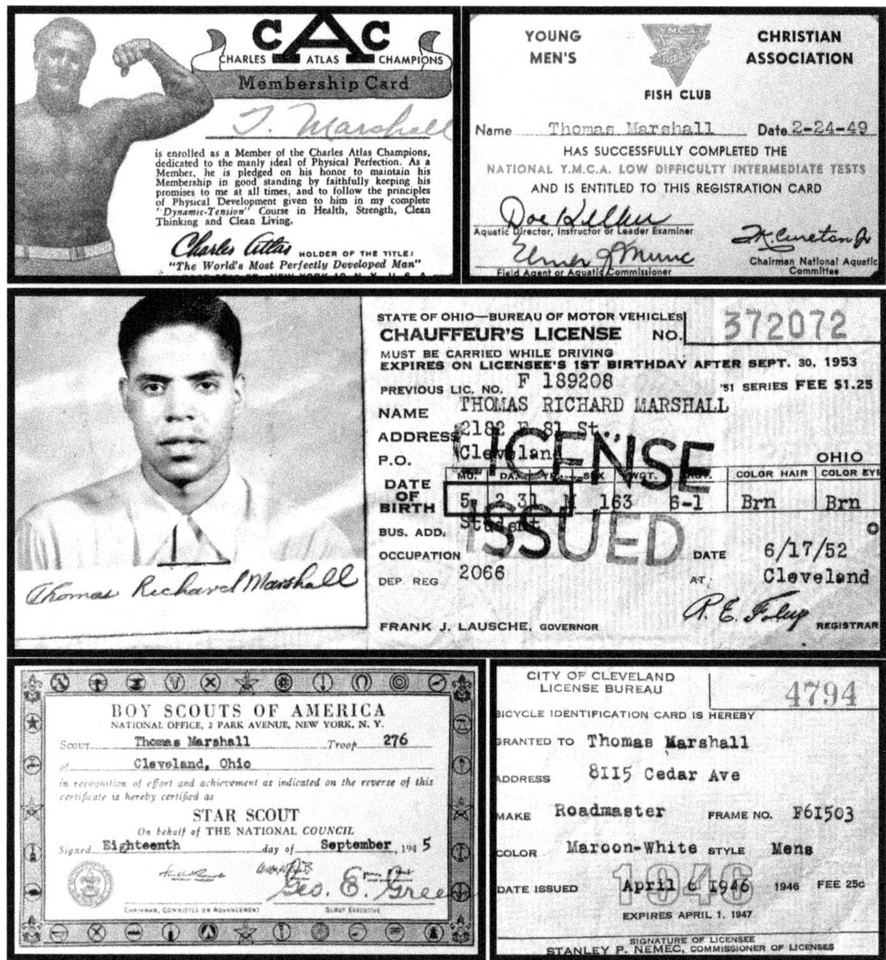

CAC
CHARLES ATLAS CHAMPIONS
Membership Card

T. Marshall

is enrolled as a Member of the Charles Atlas Champions, dedicated to the manly ideal of Physical Perfection. As a Member, he is pledged on his honor to maintain his Membership in good standing by faithfully keeping his promises to me at all times, and to follow the principles of Physical Development given to him in my complete "Dynamic-Tension" Course in Health, Strength, Clean Thinking and Clean Living.

Charles Atlas HOLDER OF THE TITLE: "The World's Most Perfectly Developed Man"

YOUNG MEN'S CHRISTIAN ASSOCIATION
FISH CLUB

Name Thomas Marshall Date 2-24-49
HAS SUCCESSFULLY COMPLETED THE
NATIONAL Y.M.C.A. LOW DIFFICULTY INTERMEDIATE TESTS
AND IS ENTITLED TO THIS REGISTRATION CARD

Aquatic Director, Instructor or Leader Examiner
Field Agent or Aquatic Commissioner
Chairman National Aquatic Committee

STATE OF OHIO—BUREAU OF MOTOR VEHICLES
CHAUFFEUR'S LICENSE NO. 372072
MUST BE CARRIED WHILE DRIVING
EXPIRES ON LICENSEE'S 1ST BIRTHDAY AFTER SEPT. 30, 1953
PREVIOUS LIC. NO. F 189208 '51 SERIES FEE $1.25
NAME THOMAS RICHARD MARSHALL
ADDRESS 2182 E. 81 St.,
P.O. Cleveland OHIO
DATE OF BIRTH 5 2 31 M 163 6-1 Brn Brn
BUS. ADD.
OCCUPATION Student DATE 6/17/52
DEP. REG 2066 AT Cleveland
LICENSE ISSUED
FRANK J. LAUSCHE, GOVERNOR
R. E. Foley REGISTRAR

Thomas Richard Marshall

BOY SCOUTS OF AMERICA
NATIONAL OFFICE, 2 PARK AVENUE, NEW YORK, N. Y.
Scout Thomas Marshall Troop 276
of Cleveland, Ohio
in recognition of effort and achievement as indicated on the reverse of this certificate is hereby certified as
STAR SCOUT
On behalf of THE NATIONAL COUNCIL
Signed Eighteenth day of September, 1945
Geo. E. Gree
Chairman, Committee on Advancement
Scout Executive

CITY OF CLEVELAND
LICENSE BUREAU 4794
BICYCLE IDENTIFICATION CARD IS HEREBY
GRANTED TO Thomas Marshall
ADDRESS 8115 Cedar Ave
MAKE Roadmaster FRAME NO. F61503
COLOR Maroon-White STYLE Mens
DATE ISSUED April 6 1946 1946 FEE 25c
EXPIRES APRIL 1, 1947
SIGNATURE OF LICENSEE
STANLEY P. NEMEC, COMMISSIONER OF LICENSES

Thomas Marshall's miscellaneous certificates that he saved in cigar boxes while in Cleveland, Ohio, 1945-1952. Donated to his children by his wife Virginia.

I got to travel the world with my third wife and childhood friends - the Fitches, the Freemans, and the Reeves. We flew and cruised to: London, Paris, Brazil, Argentina, Spain, Portugal, Morocco,

Hong Kong, Bali, Greece, Turkey, New Zealand, Mazatlan, Nova Scotia, the Blue Danube countries, Panama Canal, as well as Hawaii several times for my Iron Man Triathlons.

I became a doctor during difficult racial times in America. I was lucky. My parents successfully instilled in me the idea that I could do anything I wanted to do... and I did it all!

I have most definitely always been a proud black man, and even more than a little cocky about it. Can you tell from my stories? I was brought up during segregated times, but in Cleveland, there were so many different races at my schools, that I feel I got along well with everyone. I really don't believe that I experienced racism in the military, medical school, or in the hospitals in which I worked. If it was there, I chose not to acknowledge it! My motto, like my ex-wife Mary's, has always been "Just do it."

I taught my children by example, if not by word, to strive for excellence and to never let other people keep them from reaching their goals. I always did precisely what I wanted to do, when I wanted to do it. I did not have a "race card" chip on my shoulder like most Afro-Americans who have experienced prolonged racism. I was lucky.

And I cherished every sunset, redwood forest, lake and ocean that I laid eyes upon. Indeed, I had a superb life!

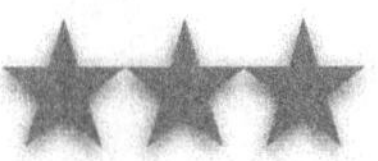

[Author's note: Dr. Thomas Richard Marshall died January 22, 2014, in Carmichael, California, at the age of 83. He provided us all with an excellent example of working hard, being confident, enjoying life's bounty, and living authentically.]

The ancestors are smiling!

Chapter 10: It Takes a Family

From the Mouth of Kathy Lynne Marshall

Kanika Marshall in her studio showroom, Elk Grove, California
Photographer: Kurt Edward Fishback, 2016

"My kids directed my life. Because I had three children, I went into the education field to be off work during the summer. The next thing was my kids getting me started in watercolor by buying me a little set of watercolors. Kathy got me started in doing art shows. My mom's legacy is the eight glasses that Norma gave her. The happiest time in my life was when my kids were grown, about from the age of 40 to the present."

- Mary Ellen Marshall, "Reflections from a Mother's Heart"

"What are those tiny lights floating in the air?" I asked my cousin Julie, who I just met for the first time in my life.

"Haven't you ever seen fireflies before?" she responded, in her charming slight mid-western drawl.

When dusk muted the sun's rays on that humid summer night in July 1966, my sister, brother and I began to see lighted objects flitting about in the air, right in front of our eyes! We tried to catch the gleaming fairies inside our cupped hands, and once we were successful, we would carefully open our hands just a smidgen to peer inside at those miraculous, phosphorescent beings, which tickled the inside of our palms. We lived in California, the Disneyland home of Tinkerbell; however, we didn't imagine that fairies really existed. But here they were in little Mount Vernon, near the center of Ohio!

Three days prior, my mom, sister, brother and I packed our clothes in brown paper bags for a three-day, cross-country adventure on the sleek California Zephyr passenger train. On the first day, the train traveled from Sacramento, south to Los Angeles, California, then east through the dry, grey-beige, high desert of Nevada. As the sun set on that first day, we marveled at the white expanse of salt flats through Salt Lake City in Utah, which gleamed brightly in the deep blue hues of the nighttime sky.

We could only afford the cheapest seats on the train. That meant sleeping in an uncomfortable sitting up position in our chairs for two very long nights. We were far from being rich people, so mom brought most of our food with us in brown grocery bags. Thankfully, she let us eat breakfast in the bright and shiny dining car, because the milk was cold and fresh there, perfect for our little boxes of cereal.

The nearly floorless space between train cars was so noisy and so very scary, because you could see the ground racing underneath between the constantly moving floor plates. That is, if you were brave enough to look down. We kids loved running from one end of the long train to the other, all day long: from our passenger car, through the bathroom car, then the dining car, then more passenger cars, then a fancy lounge car, then the dome car, then another lounge car, then cars with fancier seats, all the way to the caboose. From the caboose, we could look back upon the tracks, extending way, way out into the distance. It wasn't until later that I learned my paternal grandfather, Austin Marshall, was a Pullman porter who got to ride trains everyday for a living. Boy, was he lucky!

Sitting in the sunny glass-ceilinged dome car we had a view like none other; especially magnificent were the sunset-colored Rocky Mountains as we sped through Colorado. We young kids had to be very quiet and grown up sitting in the popular dome car, or we would be kicked out. Nebraska and Iowa whizzed by as we ran from one end of the train to the other the second day, while mom sat quietly in her chair reading, drawing anonymous face portraits, and doing crossword puzzles. She guarded our rather pitiful worldly possessions.

I was the oldest, so it was my responsibility to ensure that my 3-year-old brother and 7-year-old sister made it back to mom safe and sound, and especially without complaints from the other passengers and crew.

We kids were so excited to be visiting our Ohio family for the first time in our lives! It was dusk on our third day as we saw the city lights of Chicago, Illinois. In the massive high-ceilinged Union Station, the odor instantly reminded me of my grandfather Austin's sweet-smelling cigars. Mom bought us rum butter Lifesavers and Necco candy for the last phase of our trip. We had to ascend steps to the rickety, deep green, "Philadelphia Flyer" train, I believe it was called. As one of my favorite old broad actresses, Bette Davis, said, "it's going to be a bumpy night." That train bounced so noisily and forcefully all the way to Marion, Ohio, that we thought sure it would break down and toss us out onto the moonlit Ohio cornfields! But we made it in one piece! Mom's brother, Sonny, picked us up in his 1957 Chevy and drove us to mom's hometown of Mount Vernon.

We primarily stayed with my grandma, Pearl Williams Carter. Our cousins Julie, Everett, Roy and Jeff visited and played with us for many days, as our mother relished chatting with her mother, sisters, brothers and cousins all day and all night long. My cousin Jeff (middle of photo) was very volatile and bullying (we later found out he really had actual, serious, mental challenges). I made a deal with Jeff that if he discontinued

The Marshalls visit their Ohio family for the first time, Mt. Vernon, 1966, Photographer: Kathy Marshall

pummeling us everyday, I would teach him how to make scrumptious fried potatoes; it worked perfectly to curb his impulsive need to chase and hit us. It is true that food can soothe the savage beast (hmmm, or is it music that soothes…? Anyway, fried potatoes worked!)

There were so many differences in Mount Vernon from our west-coast home in Sacramento. A huge coal stove presided in the middle of grandma's living room; in California, everyone that we knew had more modern homes with central heating and air conditioning. We had to walk around that huge, hot stove to reach the kitchen, bathroom and staircase; and don't accidentally touch it as you pass by unless you want burns! There was also an old pitted, white, clay-footed tub upstairs, which I always feared would walk away with me, on its lion feet, while I was taking a bath! The wallpaper in that bathroom was peeling terribly. We all volunteered to strip decades of old wallpaper and paint off the walls and replace it with pretty new paper for Grandma Carter.

We were also astonished that there were no fences in the backyard. How do you keep pets and little kids from running away? Everybody in California has a proper fence that clearly delineates your property from your neighbors. Mom wanted to show off her hometown, so we went downtown and bought two pieces of candy for a penny in the candy store. At a fragrant bakery is where we first tasted the heaven that is fluffy chocolate eclairs.

Most of our days were spent at the large park down the long street from Grandma Carter's house, at 101 Walnut Street. This was the same park where our mother, and her brothers and sisters had spent their childhood years, with mom beating other kids at marbles and at basketball. They had the tallest swings we had ever seen! These were the things I remember most about the small town in the center of Ohio where our mother had been raised. She lived there until marriage whisked her away to cities along the Pacific Ocean, 2,400 miles away from her loving family.

For the second week of our Ohio vacation, we took a Greyhound bus north, to Cleveland, Ohio, where I had been born nine years prior. We would stay with our father's mother, my formidable grandma, Daisy Dooley Marshall. She was raising her daughter Shirley Jean's children - Michal, Caroline and Lori Chick - who were the same age as us. We were able to spend a considerable amount of quality time with them and we had so much fun! Michal and I became longtime pen-pals.

As petite as Grandma Daisy was, at 5' tall, she was a powerful woman! After all, she was once a licensed Embalmer and Assistant Funeral Director from 1939 to 1950 in the Marshall Funeral Home. Dad's family lived in that Funeral Home. His not-so-funny story of his mom chasing him upstairs with a cleaver in her hand was disturbing, to say the least. Thankfully, when we visited Grandma Daisy in 1966, she was living in a three-story shotgun house and her cleaver was safely inside her kitchen drawer! Later, Grandma

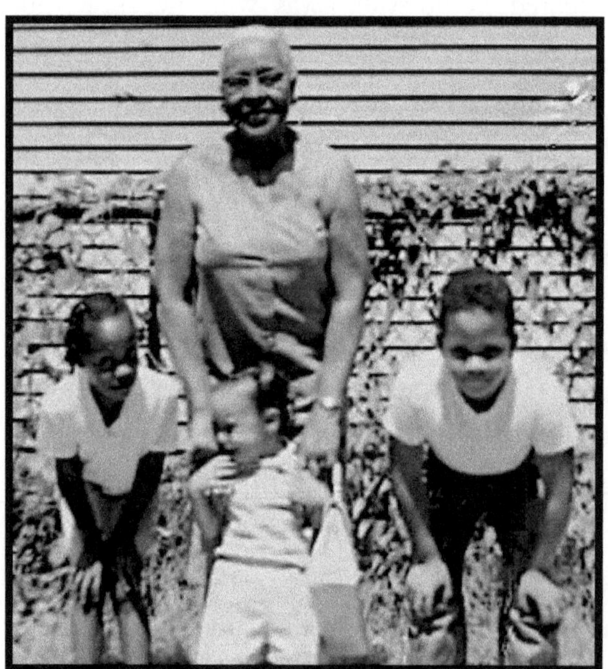

Caroline Chick, grandma Daisy Dooley, Lori and Michal Chick, Cleveland, Ohio, 1966

Daisy became a licensed practical nurse and worked for University Hospitals until she retired in 1964.

Our grandfather, Austin Marshall, had been a Pullman porter for much of his adult life, traveling on the trains most days out of every month. He had remarried and was living in his hometown of Columbus, Georgia, with his pretty second wife Vernelle.

I can still remember every morning at grandma's having to drink a spoon full of castor oil and washing away the taste with orange juice. To keep us busy, grandma enrolled all of us kids in swimming lessons at the African American YMCA,[38] where our dad had been a lifeguard during his teenage years in the 1940s. That pool was big enough for competitive swim meets and we had lessons in the deep end, where the water was so very cold! We learned to tread water for dear life to keep from sinking and to keep warm!

We really enjoyed the evenings in Cleveland where everyone on East Boulevard sat outside on the porch swing, enjoying the balmy summer weather with a glass of sweet tea. Neighbors would yell across the street to each other about the latest gossip, while we kids played hide and seek under the dim street lights. It was a charming and relaxing way to end each day.

Mom had lived with Grandma Daisy for the first six months of my life, while dad was finishing up Medical School at Ohio State College. He was two hours south of Cleveland, in Columbus, the State Capitol. Even though Grandma Daisy was sometimes very curt, mom had a warm place in her heart for how welcoming her mother-in-law and father-in-law had always been to her. Dad barely graduated from medical school because he had a hard time focusing on his studies. He knew he had a young wife and child two hours away from his school, yet he had a difficult medical curriculum to absorb and pass. Dad's medical internship and residency, in addition to his delayed military service requirements, took his young family to Seattle, Washington, in 1958, where my sister, Carrie, was born a year later. Dad learned to sail a boat, which became one of his lifelong loves. The Navy sent Lieutenant Marshall down to San Diego, California, in 1961. He had even more fun with water sports at Camp Pendleton, along with his medical duties. Having completed his military requirement, we moved to French Camp, CA, in 1963, where Greg was born. My favorite memory was climbing the gnarled weeping willow tree near our triplex. The wise old tree let me pass the hours watching the neighbor kids play, and hospital staff go to and from work. I swore to my sister that there was a family of little people living in the building across the street, whom I spied from my lofty perch, but I couldn't prove it.

Lt. Thomas Marshall, San Diego, CA, 1962

When dad finished his medical residency and internship, he was ready to open his first private practice. In 1964, he chose a one-story medical office complex in South Sacramento. One year later, he purchased a $16,000 brand new house for his family in the Larchmont Riviera area on the far east side of Sacramento City, far away from the black community in South Sacramento. Mom would often drive us back and forth to visit with her friends with whom she played contract bridge, tennis and golf.

Our immediate family was a very important part of our lives, since everybody else lived in Ohio. Our family unit included dad, mom, me, younger sister Carrie, and younger brother Greg.

Kathy, Greg, Mary and Carrie Marshall, Sacramento, California, 1974

I have so many happy, fun, but sometimes emotionally draining memories of our childhood years. Dad was a wonderful doctor and very fun-loving with his friends and running and bicycling buddies, but he was not always patient with, or kind to, the people he lived with. Our parents divorced in 1966 when I was nine years old, due to irreconcilable differences.

Mom had no money for luxuries for several years, only receiving $425 a month from dad which had to cover: the mortgage, food, utilities, clothes, gasoline, school supplies - everything. But thankfully, we had a talented mother, who grew up very poor in material things but rich in spirit thanks to her mother, Pearl Carter. We always had pencils, pens, crayons, recycled paper, cheap fabric, and yarn for us to create everything we needed. If we wanted to give someone a birthday or Christmas present, we had to use our creativity and problem-solving skills to find materials around the house and make a gift. Reduce, reuse, and recycle were our unspoken mottos back in the day! We crocheted mufflers and hats, sewed stuffed animals and our own clothes with our handy, dandy, J.C. Penny sewing machine. We also made greeting cards, pen and ink drawings and posters, hand drawn gift wrap, home-baked cookies, etc. We learned to make something from almost nothing. The lack of material things really worked to our benefit in the long run because it gave us the skills to easily see many possible, creative solutions to many of life's problems. We kids all know almost instinctively how to engineer and implement a plan of action to achieve our goals. I imagine this was much like the skills our enslaved ancestors utilized every day just for survival.

As I got older, my sensitivity to racial inequalities really began to bubble to the surface. I noticed there were only two pages in our history books about Black folk in America and they were only about slavery. Didn't Black people contribute anything positive to society? The Civil Rights movement was in full force as I entered the integrated and troubled Hiram Johnson High School in 1972. There were daily uprisings and fights between the black, white, Asian and Hispanic students at our school.

"Say it loud, I'm Black and I'm Proud!" was our black students' motto. We proudly wore our thick black Afro hair styles with a cake cutter sticking out of the top of our hair. We wore vividly patterned jersey shirts, the-shorter-the-better hot pants,[39] big hoop earrings and thick-soled Famolare[40] shoes. We watched the "Soooouuullll Train"[41] music TV show on Saturdays. After being denigrated as a race for so many centuries in this country and around the world, we just enjoyed being Black!

The Black Panther Party for Self-Defense was the leader in this newly proclaimed Black self-love fest. They practiced militant self-

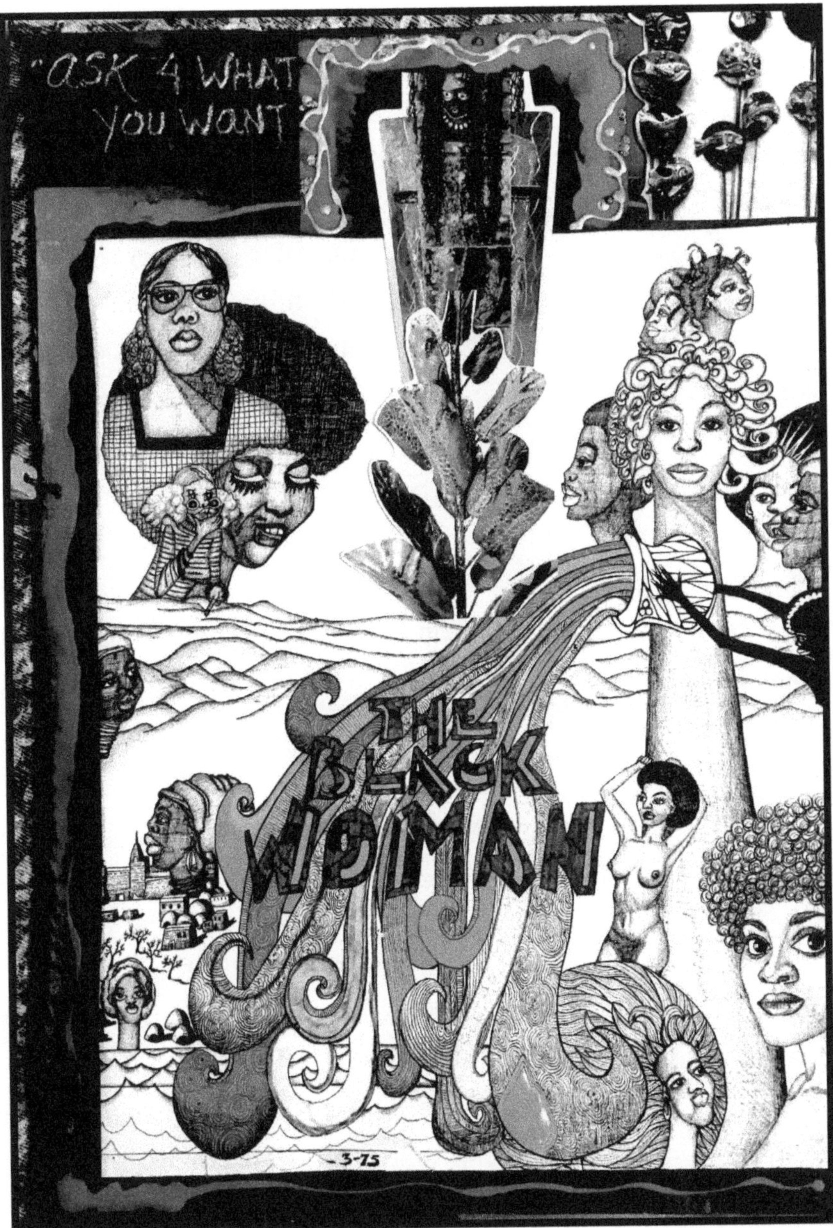

Kathy Marshall's teenage Afrocentric art, Sacramento, California, 1975

defense of minority communities against the U.S. government, and fought to establish revolutionary socialism through mass organizing and community based programs.[42] However, the newspapers rarely covered their positive food and education programs for poor and black people. Newspapers only covered the fear mongering stories about "uppity Negroes" with guns. During this exciting and difficult period of civil unrest, though, my blossoming artwork became 100% Afrocentric.[43] I made colorful posters for Black History Month for various schools and Black organizations. My militant feelings grew and grew the more I found out about slavery and Jim Crow-like segregation that existed in many parts of the country (then and now). I wanted to be *black enough.*

My college career started at Sacramento City College in January 1975, after graduating mid-term from high school. I felt like a bird soaring, free at last! It was wonderful to be taking classes that interested me, like African American History and Women's Studies. We were openly talking about topics that would have gotten our black ancestors lynched, but we loved the freedom of expression! Can you dig it?

I worked hard to get a two-year Associate of Arts degree in just three semesters, while maintaining a respectable 3.64 grade point average, and working part-time jobs at the college and a department store. I wanted, no, I needed to prove to myself that I *was* smart enough, contrary to the negative-speak and demeaning treatment I received from my father as a child.

The bi-centennial year of our country, 1976, was a huge year for me. I was fortunate to get a full-time, entry-level clerical job filing accident reports with the Department of the California Highway Patrol, earning a whopping $525 per month! I was truly free now to live life on my own terms! That same year, I transferred to Sacramento State College, initially pursuing an International Business degree; later, a French degree.

I had my own money to buy a brand new Panama Brown Volkswagen Rabbit car for $100 per month, and I rented a one-bedroom apartment, in the diverse Oak Park neighborhood of Sacramento, for $125. It was the perfect job for a full-time college student, and most of my swing-shift coworkers also went to college during the day, like I did.

But then a Love Bird dive-bombed me in August 1976. My coworker, Phyllis, told me that she wanted to introduce me to her sister-in-law, Lovey Anderson, who was a Manager with the Employment Development Department. So the next day, I curled my long dark hair in the popular Farrah Fawcett, feathered-shag hairstyle;[44] I hoped the heat of the day wouldn't frizz it up before our after-work meeting at 11 PM. I wore a new gauze shirt and decent slacks to work, for once, and tried not to sweat during my 8-hour work shift. Work was finally over and we drove two blocks from our office to Lovey's house, at 26th and W Streets. I was so nervous! We rang the bell and waited a few heartbeats. The door opened and out stepped a fine brother man who looked kind of like Malcolm X. Our eyes met and, I kid you not, there were sparks flashing every which way in that star-filled night sky! Phyllis saw it, he saw it, and my red face showed it. Boom de Boom de Blam Blam! He and I had made a connection unlike any I had ever had in my 19 years on this Earth.

But what clenched the deal was what happened next… Phyllis and I went into their compact house. I was formally introduced to her nephew, Kenneth Wayne Anderson, and his mother, Lovetta "Lovey", and father, Charles "Chuck" Anderson. After a little chitchat, we decided to play the game "MasterMind." Without me seeing his choices, Ken selected four colored pegs from six possible colors and inserted them one after another onto a peg board. Like the game of Battleship, I had to guess which colored peg was in the first position, which was second, and so forth. Believe it or not, I guessed ALL of the colors he selected in the CORRECT position on my FIRST guess! Were we made for each other or what? We had it bad, real bad for each other. We only saw each other on weekends at my little apartment, though, until he got a job with the Pacific Gas and Electric Company in Sacramento, repairing all of their vehicles.

After living together for two years, "I" popped the question and Ken became my husband in 1979. We got married in a very simple ceremony in his parent's lush backyard garden, on a 105-degree day. My Grandmother Daisy had flown out from Ohio to participate in the wedding, but dad did not arrive on time and we had to proceed without them. My brother, Greg, gave me away. It was the 1970s and I, an obvious feminist, kept my maiden name. I also kept a firm grip on my new husband's arm as I took my first plane ride, flying down to Los Angeles for our honeymoon. His favorite cousins, Steven and Dorisse Jones, arranged for us to stay in the extravagant, golden-mirrored, Bonaventure Hotel on the 18th floor, which had superb views of Los Angeles. What a dream Honeymoon!

We bought our first house in the Golf Course Terrace area of South Sacramento with our wedding gift money. I soon got out of the clerical field and got a job in the CHP's first mainframe computer room. Yes, 1979 was a huge year for us: we married, I was 22 and he was 29, we purchased our first house, and I earned a totally non-useful Bachelor of Arts degree in French. Always wanting to learn and be busy, though, I decided to take fun college classes in 1980 and 1981, like clay pottery and sculpture classes. I also took the opportunity to learn Spanish, which was a much more useful language in California. My wise mother encouraged me to get a Masters Degree before getting wrapped up with kids. Being a respectful daughter, I did just that, earning a Masters degree in Public Administration at night school in 1983, while working full-time during the days at CHP.

Shortly after our marriage, Ken became a firefighter and within two years had promoted to Captain with the Sacramento Fire Department. Soon he assumed the role of Training Instructor, teaching newly-hired people (including my brother Greg in 1986) to become excellent firefighters. Within ten years of being in the Department, Ken was an Acting Chief. We were living the American Dream, with a 3,400 square-foot house on one-third of an acre in the choice Pocket Area in Sacramento. We were able to travel and go to restaurants whenever we wanted. He bought nice suits and a fancy Lincoln Town car, etc. Every day of my life I gave (and still give) homage to my ancestors for never giving up the struggle in the face of perpetual racism and inequalities so that we can "Live The Dream"[45] with a lot of hard work on our part and a little luck.

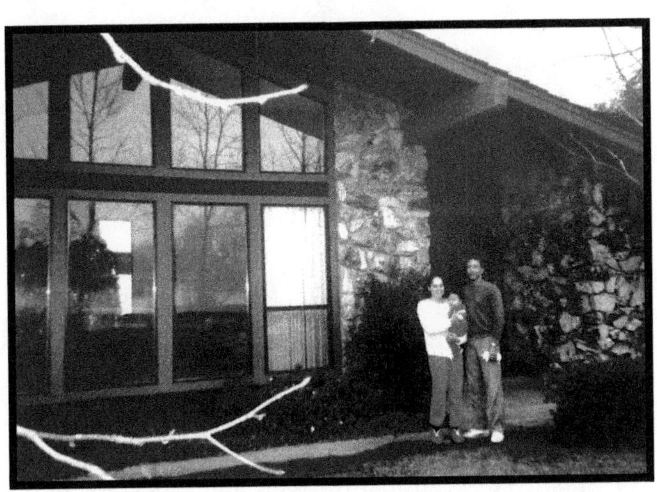

Anderson-Marshall family home at 7640 Greenhaven Drive, Sacramento, California, 1986

After a few years of blissful marriage, I banished the fear that I might repeat dad's spotty parenting style and gave in to having the children that Ken and my in-laws had wanted for so long. We had our first son, Isaac Charles Anderson, in 1985, when I was 28 and Ken was 35. Our second son, Matthew Thomas Anderson, was born in 1990.

Matthew, Kathy, Ken, and Isaac, Sacramento, CA, 1991

Isaac Charles was named for his paternal great-grandfather Isaac Anderson, and his paternal grandfather Charles Anderson. Matthew Thomas Anderson was named for his maternal grandfather Thomas Marshall. Unfortunately, the bubble burst after 18 years of a generally very positive relationship. Ken and I had to divorce in 1994 due to an unrelenting addiction that consumed him, lost our dream house, and destroyed our family unit. Four years later, he had kicked the habit and was regaining his life. Unfortunately, he was killed by a drunk driver in 1998, leaving our children fatherless and me a single mother. It was truly a great loss to our family and to humanity, one which saddens me to this day. I began living the excruciatingly difficult life that beset my grandmother Carter, and my mother: being a single parent.

Our oldest son, Isaac, was an extremely lively, inventive child, who is an excellent creative writer. I know that because instead of spanking him, I gave him creative writing assignments to work off his punishment(s); he had so many stories that I was able to publish a book of his writings! (smile)

Isaac joined the Marine Corps in his senior year at Laguna Creek High School in Elk Grove, earning a high security clearance job working with computers. Isaac was stationed in Iraq during the beginning of the Iraq War and let me tell you, I refused to watch the negative war news on TV during that scary 13-month period of his service there. After several promotions during a ten-year period, Isaac eventually became a Gunnery Sergeant in the Marine Corps at the age of 31, then a Drill Instructor in San Diego, California.

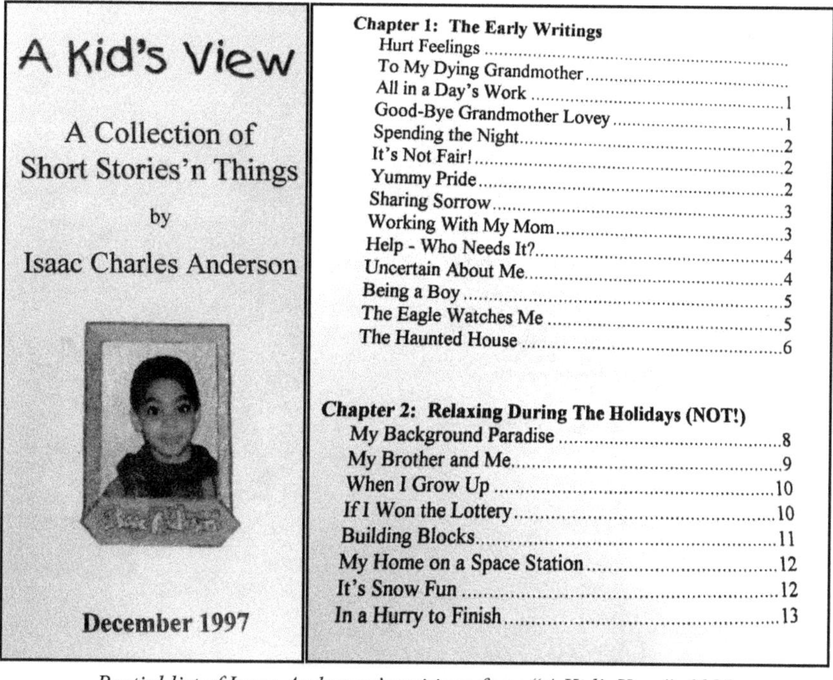

A Kid's View

A Collection of Short Stories'n Things

by

Isaac Charles Anderson

December 1997

Chapter 1: The Early Writings

Chapter 2: Relaxing During The Holidays (NOT!)

Partial list of Isaac Anderson's writings from "A Kid's View", 1997

Isaac married his lovely and accomplished high school sweetheart, Jameillah LeChé Davis, when he was 20 and she 19 years old. They purchased their first house in North Carolina and a second, seven years later. They brought into the world my three darling grandchildren: Jazmine LynAnn in 2008, Isaiah Christian in 2010, and Jeremiah Liam Anderson in 2016.

In 2011, Isaac's military orders took him and his family to Okinawa, Japan, for three years. I was fortunate to be able to visit them in that fascinating Japanese island that is overrun by American military bases. Truly, the local people are humble and courteous, and love cute bright happy colors. I got my first (and only) two tattoos there.

Isaac's orders brought them back to their house near Camp LeJeune, in Jacksonville, North Carolina, for another three years. Being present for the birth of their third child in April 2016, it was my job to keep the older grandkids occupied during the difficult labor process. I kept them calm while they were witnessing the amazing birth of their brand new brother at 3:33 AM. That experience was one of the highlights of my life! In 2015, Isaac found Jesus and his family joined a church which

Jameillah, Jeremiah, Isaac, Jazmine, Isaiah Anderson, Photographer: Marissa Marquez (Photos by Marissa), 2017

gave them the inner peace they were seeking. Each time we visit each other, I am so gratified to see Isaac playing with, and teaching, his children some of the things that I tried to teach him. My mother had taught us what had been passed down to her from her parents, an unbroken line from the ancestors.

Matthew Anderson earning his first blackbelt in Taekwondo, 2010

My second son, Matthew Thomas Anderson, was born to become Isaac's playmate in 1990. He was such a calming influence for our entire family. I'll never forget Isaac constantly saying "Watch me, watch me, Matthew, this is how you do it" when teaching his younger brother how to do cartwheels, or ride a bike, or successfully navigate a skateboard.

Matthew decided to take a different course of action for his life. He joined the Franklin High School band, playing the quints (five different-sized, tenor drums attached around his waist). He was in the marching band, symphonic band, and drum line. He definitely got the percussion skills from his father, who used to play the timbales and other Afro-latin drums. Matthew graduated from Franklin High School with honors, obtained an Associate of Arts degree from Cosumnes River College, then earned a Bachelor of Science degree in Computer Science from Sacramento State

University. He was able to get a student intern job while still going to college, obtaining a permanent position at the Department of Motor Vehicles. He became a Staff Programmer Analyst within two years of obtaining his college degree. In 2017, he decided to go back to school for a Masters Degree in Computer Science from Sacramento State University. Matthew saved his pennies, like his enslaved ancestors did, and was able to purchase his first home at the age of 23.

Taekwondo has been one of Matthew's loves since 1998, when I enrolled him and his brother in taekwondo to help them during the grieving process for their father, who had been hit by a drunk driver. Over the years, both boys enjoyed lessons at the Sacramento Taekwondo Club. After brother Isaac entered the Marines, Matthew went on to achieve his first-degree black belt in 2010, and achieved a second degree blackbelt in 2015. He also represented the United States as the 2015-2016 National Taekwondo Freestyle Champion, after having won gold medals in Taekwondo Championships in Texas and Colorado.

I am a very proud mother of both sons!

My two boys are very different individuals, although they played together very well as children. Isaac gave in to his every whim and did whatever he wanted to do whenever he wanted to do it (like his grandpa Tom!). On the other hand, Matthew played the "mommy game" doing what he was supposed to do, when he was asked to do it. I'll leave it to your imagination as to which one had an easier time growing up in my predictable, low-requirements household! (smile)

Isaac and Matthew grew up in the small town of Elk Grove, California, where racial diversity reigned, so they did not really understand the importance of studying black history. They did not really appreciate the sacrifices that our ancestors made for them in this country. In a way, it is great that my sons have not experienced much racism and that they have good friends of all nationalities. How fabulous is it that my sons saw the successful eight years of the first black President, Barack Obama, from 2009 to 2016! I still try to explain to them why it is so important that they are ever-vigilant in exercising the hard-won voting, employment, and housing rights for which so many of our black ancestors fought and died.

I was so very thankful to be able to retire early from the California Highway Patrol in 2012, at the age of 55. I had enjoyed serving as a Personnel Selection Consultant and Manager of the Department's Selection Research Program.

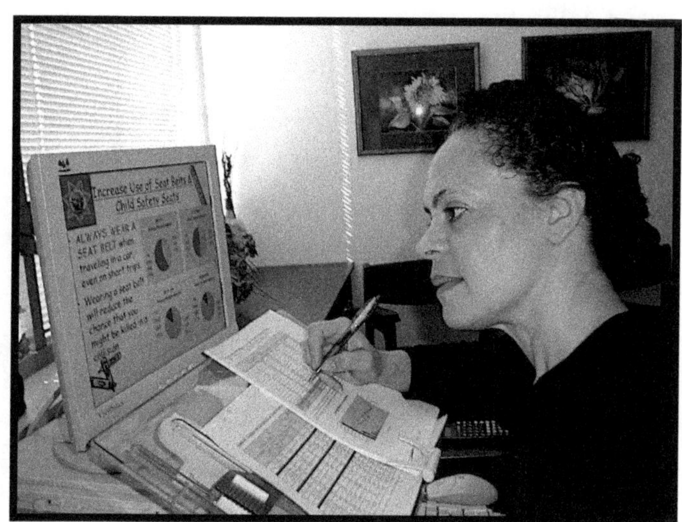

Kathy Marshall working at California Highway Patrol Personnel Office, West Sacramento, CA, c. 2009

However, I had been working there for 36 years and was ready to live the third stage of my life: the American Dream. The true Dream, I think, is to have enough money and good health to be able to do whatever you want to do whenever you want to do it in retirement. I was so ready!

I had started my Kanika African Sculptures art business in 1993, after taking many clay classes from 1990 to 1993. The business fed my soul, as well as my children, after the divorce in 1994. Taking ceramic and sculpture art classes in the 1980s and 1990s, and recycled steel welding classes after 2010, helped me to create a distinctive collection of mixed-media Kanika African Sculptures. I have been fortunate to sell enough art to appease my ego and my pocketbook, by selling my sculptures in stores, at art shows, to the City of Elk Grove's permanent art collection, to all nine members of California's Black Caucus, and to many hundreds of customers in California and worldwide. Selling my art helped me through many difficult financial times, but also boosted me egoistically through winning numerous competitive awards. I have always maintained that the ancestors work joyously through my fingers to help create each distinctive art piece.

"Mz. Tutu" Kinetic Sculpture by Kanika Marshall, 2016

Quite frankly, I was tired of actively selling art. Working a full-time for 36 years, while being a full-time single parent, and working 15 to 20 hours every week for 23 years on my art business, I was tired. It is exhausting even thinking about the huge amount of time marketing, maintaining a website, Facebook page, and a newsletter. The biggest difficulty, though, was lifting and transporting my large, heavy, welded steel and clay sculptures to and from art shows and galleries. My aging body forced me to slow way down, and now I prefer to sell my work in my home sculpture garden.

The ancestors began calling me to write their stories in October 2016. They wanted their history to live on indefinitely and they needed my help to do it. When the ancestors call, I listen!

From the Mouth of Carrie Marshall Malenab

I was born in Seattle, Washington, in 1959, when my dad was doing his one-year medical internship. Spending time with family and friends is my true joy, especially if there is water and a warm sandy beach nearby. My daily goal in life is to love others and honor God. While growing up, my sister called me the angel because, "She was so nice, happy, and had a large circle of good friends who adored her."

I always worked hard in school. I was fortunate to earn a nearly full-ride scholarship to Pepperdine University in Malibu, California, where I had the opportunity to study in West Germany during the 1977-78 school year. I transferred to Scripps College in Claremont, California, and completed my Bachelor of Arts degree in International Relations in 1980.

After graduating from college, I married my high school sweetheart and worked for Volkswagen of America in Culver City, California. On December 15, 1981, I was blessed with my own angel, Lauren Elise McGhee. Unfortunately, drug abuse was a huge problem in California in the 1970's and 1980's, and very soon my husband's problem caused us to divorce. My daughter and I returned to Sacramento to live in an apartment close to my childhood home where I rededicated my life to God and restarted my life. My mother, brother, and sister were, and always have been, a wonderful support system for us.

To make additional money, I began selling Mary Kay Cosmetics and created my own sewing business, along with working full-time at McLaren Engineering. McLaren is a subcontractor for Aerojet, which is an aerospace firm. In 1985, wanting my work to have a greater impact in the world, especially with young people, I went back to school to earn my teaching credential, while continuing to work full time, as a single parent.

I taught at Carriage Elementary and Sylvan Middle School in the San Juan School District. After 11 years, to be closer to home, I took a job at T. R. Smedberg Middle School in the Elk Grove School District. I eventually taught social science and AVID at Sheldon High School prior, to earning my Masters degree in Educational Administration. I worked for nine years as a Vice Principal at Pleasant Grove High School, prior to retiring.

During the busy time in my life, I became an active member of the Alpha Kappa Alpha Sorority, Incorporated, the first African American Sorority dedicated to service to all mankind.

I also met my real Romeo, who lived in my apartment complex. Romeo Faustino Malenab, was born in the Philippines and immigrated to California in 1977, after waiting eight years to obtain the proper immigration approvals. He served in the United States Air Force, both active and reserve. Greatly appreciating the American Dream, he was able to purchase cars and a home in 1985 while he worked in the Operations Department of Sacramento's nuclear power plant, part of the Sacramento Metropolitan Utilities District. Romeo and I married in 1990, and Lauren and I became a part of his large, loving, Filipino family.

Twenty-eight years later, I fell in love again when I welcomed my precious grandson, E'Drece Brian Walls, into the world on October 16, 2008. Romeo and I are having a wonderful time being retired grandparents and pouring our lives into E'Drece.

But this book is also about our memories growing up, right? After thinking a bit, I came up with the following notable events that stand out in my mind, in no particular order of prominence or chronology.

Soothing the Savage Beast

When we visited our Ohio family for the first time in 1966, we stayed for a week at our grandmother Carter's house in Mount Vernon. We met for the first time several of our first cousins who visited us during that week. Cousin Jeff Carter was a wild man, always chasing us and acting crazy. I remember my sister bribing him with homemade fried potatoes, which he loved. She said she would teach him how to make them himself, but only if he stopped beating us up. They both were nine years old at the time. Kathy patiently and cautiously taught him how to use a knife to cut the potatoes, how much oil to put in the skillet, how to light Grandma's large iron stove, how to carefully drop the cut potatoes into the hot oil, how to salt them as they were cooking, and how to use a slotted spatula to remove the browned potatoes onto paper towels, to sop up the excess grease. Jeff was a willing student and it was

Carrie and Romeo Malenab, Lauren McGhee, and E'Drece Walls, Sacramento, California, 2016

surprisingly nice to see him so excited with learning how to do something himself. The best reward, of course, was getting to eat what they made for everyone. She tamed the wild beast! Smile.

The Easy Bake Oven

We did not often get toys growing up, because mom had little extra money after she and dad divorced. But one Christmas, Santa bought Kathy and me an Easy Bake Oven! We spent many happy hours making cookies and cakes using the small pre-packaged ingredients that we mixed with water and slid into the Easy Bake Oven slot. The warmth of light bulbs served as the heating source to "bake" these delicacies. We became quite the bakers, learning in 7th grade home economics class how to make delicious cinnamon buns and all manner of cookies, cakes, pies, and omelets and dinner entrees. It is truly amazing that none of us became big as houses for all the baked goods we ate after school!

Fabric Addiction

In the junior high school home economics class for the girls, half of the year was spent teaching us how to cook and half was spent learning how to sew. Boys were taught metal shop and wood working. Kathy and I learned how to design and sew our own clothes. Being poor, mom could not buy us many clothes, so for a few lean years while she was going to college, we got our clothing from the Salvation Army. Once she became a teacher, we could buy clothes from the White Front department store. Learning how to make and customize our own clothes became a lifelong passion. My sister and I relished our trips to the Yardage Shop on Arden Way. Touching the fabrics, browsing the packages of patterns, and making decisions on what to sew and how to embellish our creations was one of our favorite pastimes! The Yardage

Shop was a bit too expensive, though, and we could only buy the cheapest fabrics and remnants there. Later, Hancock's Fabrics, in the Southgate Shopping Center, became our go-to fabric store. We could get fabric there for 50 cents per yard! I actually became more of a clothing designer in my 30s, making African-style outfits out of authentic African fabric that we bought from Hancock's and an import store down in Los Angeles. I created African hats, scarves, and two-piece outfits. I had my own clothing line, with my own label: Carrie M. Designs. I sold my African fashions at craft/vendor shows for a couple of years, next to my mother's watercolor booth, and my sister's African sculptures booth.

Starting as a Summer School Aide

One summer in junior high school, I think, we were student aides at Edison Elementary School. Those kids were so wild and so bad, we vowed never to become teachers! Of course that changed a decade later when I decided to make educating children my career.

Child Labor!

After my parents divorced in 1966, we visited our father and his new wife, Pam, every other weekend. In 1967 or 1968, dad said he had a big surprise for us, as he picked us up from mom's house. My sister, brother and I squeezed ourselves into the back seat of dad's topless, racing green, MGB convertible roadster car. We soon headed for lands unknown, with the wind whipping our thick hair around our faces. Driving along Interstate 80 past Sacramento going east, we exited the freeway about 20 minutes later onto Rocklin Road. We were in "the country" in the foothills of Placer County! Sierra College was on the left, and golden, grassy fields were all around us. We sped past low wooden fences containing horses and cows and sheep. There were lots of oak and olive trees, peach tree orchards, and pasture lands. We soon turned left onto Wells Avenue.

At a curve in the road, dad quickly turned into a gravel area and stopped the car. "This is it!" he said proudly. "This will be our new home!" Exiting the tiny car, we were surrounded by a field of unruly yellow, prickly, star-thistle weeds and free-growing grasses, about a foot tall. We learned that dad bought this 28-acre property located in the small town of Loomis. This was indeed the "country" with large parcel properties. There were no commercial establishments, such as grocery or other stores, for miles around. There was only one gasoline station for the towns of Rocklin and Loomis, and only one small, old-time general store.

Dad had contracted with noted architect, Carter Sparks, to build him an unusual, three-level, executive home on the top of the high hill. During our bi-weekly visits, we were expected to help dad use survey instruments to map out where farm fencing should be built around his property, and along the street. We were also expected to help him build a massive, double-wide wooden gate from the street to the mouth of his 200-yard-long blacktop driveway. That driveway led up a steep curving hill up to the house at the top of the hill.

Thomas Marshall's Home in Loomis California, 1969-2002

Alongside to the lower-level driveway, he had a large pit dug out to be fed by the small creek that abutted his property. This became a large rectangular lake that would eventually contain large-mouth bass and other smaller fish. It took about a year for his house to be built and it was really interesting to see the progress made each weekend we visited.

Once dad and Pam moved in, it became our normal schedule, during our bi-weekly visits, to eat a hearty breakfast of Spanish eggs, grapefruit, hot buttered toast, and orange juice at about 8:30 AM. When dad went to work at the hospital after breakfast, our difficult chores began. We were to grab two 2-gallon buckets, walk down the steep driveway to the lake, fill those buckets, and deep-water the small pine and deodar cedar trees, and juniper bushes, that dad had planted around the lake, the house, and alongside the long fence that edged the immense property.

Loomis is warm in the spring, and very hot summer and fall, so if we dawdled after breakfast, we would be doing the watering chore in the hot sun. The scratchy star-thistle weeds against our legs on the way to and from getting water from the lake felt like needles pricking our skin. Perspiration makes the pain worse, as red scratches and welts appeared on our legs. Because each prick of the skin becomes intensely itchy, oddly enough, it starts actually to feel good when your legs were scratched by more star-thistle! After giving each plant at least two full buckets of water, we were exhausted, hot, sweaty, thirsty, hungry, and very itchy. But we had one last feat to perform: walking back up that steep hill with our empty water buckets! We were pitiful, whining all the way about child labor laws! Mercifully, at the top of the hill was a 50-foot swimming pool, beckoning us to visit. What else would tired children do in that circumstance? Yes, we jumped in the pool, clothes and all!

Black Shag Carpet

Dad's second wife, Pam, had an exuberant sense of style. Remember the avocado green carpet and orange and gold wall colors from the 1970s? Well, that was too "normal" for her! She was much more avant-garde. The entire top level of dad's house was comprised of two huge rooms: a TV room with two floor-to-ceiling glass walls. The other room was his master bed and bathroom, which had one huge glass wall overlooking the pool, the expansive lake, and pine and cedar trees that dad planted and we watered. On the floors upstairs, Pam proposed having 2" tall black shag carpet installed on the entire top floor. On the lowest level, she had deep purple shag carpet installed in a sunken living room! One does not easily vacuum thick shag carpet for it could clog the vacuum rollers. No, there is a special rake that one must use. It has nubby "fingers" that gently separate the strands of shag. That was our job when we came to visit: to use that rake over the entire top level and in the sunken area downstairs. Thankfully, the middle level had black slate on the floors which was easy to mop!

The Camping Jones

My dad used to take us camping, mostly up to the redwoods in Humboldt County, near the Pacific Ocean. We used sleeping bags in dad's old Navy tent, which still smelled a bit oily from use in the 1960s when he was stationed in Seattle, Washington, and San Diego, California. We kids learned to love the outdoors and camping in general. We would even erect dad's tent in the backyard and invite our girlfriends for sleepovers! When I married Romeo, we got into the habit of camping several times a month with friends, my husband's family or his coworkers, or my family. My husband worked for SMUD and they had a special campground for employees off Ice House Road, along U.S. 50. What was so special about it was that each campsite had electrical hook ups. In the mid-1980s, it was fantastic to be able to bring coffee makers, blow dryers, and even portable TVs or blanket warmers to help make the camping experience more enjoyable. One time, we invited Ken and Kathy and their just-turned-one-year-old son, Isaac, to join us. They had a cute little pop-up tent which literally took them 30-seconds to erect, while the rest of us were dutifully sweeping debris from our campsite, unfurling our tents, raising the tent sides, and staking the edges into the ground.

From the Mouth of Gregory Forrest Marshall

Let's face facts: not to brag, but I have always been mechanically-inclined. I was born in 1963 at the San Joaquin General Hospital in French Camp, California. I have always seemed to know, almost instinctively, how to build and fix things, from as far back as I can remember.

When I was only 7 or 8, my sister Kathy said I used to make them the fluffiest egg omelettes by whipping the egg whites and folding them into the egg yolks and baking them in the oven (because I was too young to use the stove). At the age of 13, I designed and built a 5-foot tall concrete safe in my mom's garage, for my coin collection. When I was 15, I installed a security system in her home. In my later teenage years and early 20s, I tricked out (customized) several of my Volkswagen Beetle cars. I do not know where this natural mechanical and engineering ability came from, but my sister says it may have been genetically passed down to me from our enslaved ancestors who were ironworkers.

Greg Marshall, Sacramento, CA, c. late 1970s

One of my favorite memories as a child was performing gymnastics in our house while our mother was still at work [Mom, cover your ears!]. We children were not allowed to even sit on the "good" couch in the living room, let alone remove those couch cushions, put them on the floor, and do forward rolls and flips over them! But we did! We got every pillow, and couch and chair cushion, in the house and laid them end to end on the floor, in the living room and family room, to serve as a safe landing zone. We would stand in the hall bathroom, then run down the hall at full speed and tumble, roll, handspring, jump, and cartwheel over the pillows, then run through the kitchen, back down the hall to the bathroom. Round and around we went, over and over, through the house, performing death-defying feats of gymnastics. Those activities should have resulted in multiple trips to the hospital, but we survived. When we heard mom's car coming into the driveway, we scrambled to return the cushions to their rightful places and plopped down like sweet little angels, slowing our breathing, before our mother walked through the door. Thank goodness for manual garage doors which required the driver to put the car in park, get out of the car, physically open the heavy garage door, get back into the car, then drive into the garage. That gave us a couple of minutes to put everything back in place. Good times!

I also remember fondly my sister's baking skills. Whether I just got home from school or I was studying in my bedroom, the aroma of baking cinnamon rolls, granola, cookies and whatever else she was concocting during her moment of creativity, made me powerless, and I had to sample the amazing treats!

Who can forget the fun times we had at my father's country home in Loomis, California? Every other weekend at dad's house, one of our favorite chores was digging up to 6-inch rocks from the entirely rocky soil around the house. This de-rocked area would eventually become the front lawn. We would carry the dug-up rocks to an area 20-feet away, which would soon become a retaining wall around the dining room. Of course, we helped our Renaissance Man of a father build those retaining walls too. We patiently handed him rock after rock, as he mortared them into place. Dad always preferred to do tasks himself, like building walls, doing concrete work, planting trees, using a riding mower to weekly mow the lawns he planted, etc. We became the beneficiaries of how to construct rock walls, sprinkler systems, pouring concrete, etc., types of do-it-yourself projects from our industrious father.

I was also a daredevil on my bicycle, a stuntman as a baseball shortstop, and I continued our Dad's 25-year record as a bicyclist at Eppie's Great Race, which was a triathlon of running, bicycling and kayaking teams. I rode the bicycle leg on my teams.

In 1986, I joined the Sacramento Fire Department, being trained by my sister's husband, Ken Anderson, who was a Captain and Trainer at the Sacramento Fire Department's "Training Tower" for several years. When I was 23, I purchased my first house in North Sacramento, and maintained several small businesses in my spare time. You see, firefighters only work ten 24-hour days each month, leaving 20 days a month to work on hobbies and part-time businesses. I completed an

Greg Marshall, Eppie's Great Race
Photographer: Kathy Marshall, 2015

Greg Marshall's first house, Sacramento, CA, 1987

Associate of Arts degree in Fire Science then became an engineer, being responsible for maintaining the Light Plant truck for hazardous materials investigations and heavy rescue calls for service.

I also invented several tools for firefighters and developed my own design of portable meditative water fountains, as well as many other inventions. People call me MacGyver[46] because I enjoy solving complex problems by making things out of ordinary objects.

In 1994 when I was 31, I met my soulmate, Sue Walker, at a country and western dance club. She was another entrepreneur and go-getter who sold many different holistic health products, such as: aromatherapy oil and magnet therapy, in addition to her full-time job representing a baking company nationwide.

We married in 1995 and purchased my dream property in Garden Valley, a remote area in the foot hills near where gold was first discovered in California in 1849. Our compact, 1,200 square foot ranch style house was surrounded by woods and a babbling brook in the lower backyard. We had our wedding on the huge backyard deck. I was proud to say this was similar to the amazing rural hill-top property our father had for 30 years in Loomis, California.

Greg Marshall's property in Garden Valley, CA, c. 1996

After a few years, Sue and I both decided to retire from our respective day jobs, sell our individual properties, and purchase a Hypnotheraphy School together in Auburn, California. I used my building skills to retrofit the two-story building for living quarters on the second floor, as well as the office and school rooms on the bottom floor. We successfully managed the school for a few years, but then eventually decided to divorce in 2002.

Following our divorce, I became a building contractor, rehabbing houses by performing electrical, plumbing, and other home renovations for customers. I also maintained some of my health-oriented entrepreneurial businesses, as well as continuing to stay physically fit. After a while, aches and pains encouraged my body to suggest that I trade the physically taxing activity of construction work to something more cerebral, like financial services, including life insurance.

Life is good and I remain optimistic about the future.

[Author's note: The stories in this chapter were joyfully provided by me and my siblings. It was an enjoyable romp down memory lane, with lots of laughter. Good times.]

Epilogue

I am living my 60th year and feeling the pressure to ensure that my ancestors' memories are published, so their descendants and others can know them too. If I don't write about my ancestors now, who will?

It has been quite emotional re-reading my mother's journal, "*Reflections From a Mother's Heart*," and selecting passages for this book. Figuring out which personal experiences should be included brought back so many touching family memories. Searching through the 26,000 photographs stored on my smart phone was also an interesting romp down memory lane, as I tried to choose the perfect photos to illustrate the stories in this book. Having my brother and sister edit this composition, and adding their own narratives, was a bonding exercise, for sure!

Writing these stories from the point of view, and voice of each character, was not only great fun but really made the chapters come alive authentically. My father, Dr. Thomas R. Marshall, was the strongest voice; he channeled the most vivid picture of his very full life. His ultra-confident personality shines through from his enthusiastic words, daring deeds and revealing photos. I think he should have told more stories about growing up in a funeral home though …

I can hear Great-Aunt Reba Williams' favorite expression - it's the same ol' same ol' - when asked how she was feeling. I still chuckle at the rather matter-of-fact way this humble centenarian described how she felt, finally receiving her high school diploma at the age of 106!

Exceptionally gratifying to me was speaking with our eldest elder, 93-year-old Charles Williams, about his remarkable adventures as a human guinea pig for tuberculosis testing in 1946. The pride in his voice, when recounting how he successfully lobbied the Navy to be correctly classified as a "Machinist Mate" in 1943, was palpable.

I was shocked hearing that my Aunt Lavata Williams was nearly kidnapped in Istanbul, Turkey, after she and her mother, Reba, had finished visiting the Holy Land. Her account of how she was so quickly surrounded by a group of local men before she even knew what was happening, was absolutely riveting!

One of my main aims in writing this book is to encourage everyone to commemorate their own ancestors' lives and stories in writing NOW. Interview your elders and other living relatives, and write your family's stories, before it is too late. Along those lines, I am in the process of finishing up my second book, entitled *"Finding Otho: The Search for Our Enslaved Williams Family History."* Otho is the slave from whom most of the characters in this book descend. To help others research their ancestors, I shall include the many different techniques I used for breaking through the 1870 Brick Wall that many people encounter while conducting slave research. My goal is to share those techniques and results with others so they can do the same with their families. The ancestors are calling, and when they call, we should listen!

The true stories woven with the African fabric of historical events in *The Ancestors Are Smiling!* clearly illustrate the tenacity of my courageous ancestors. All ensured that each new generation had a better life than the last.

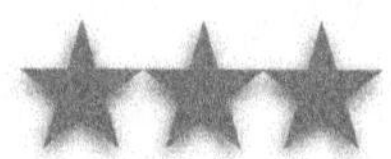

The Ancestors are Smiling!

Bibliography

Haley, Alex. *Roots: The Saga of an American Family.* USA: Doubleday Books, 1976.

Lauron, Neal C. *Celebrating a Life Well-Lived.* Columbus, Ohio: The Columbus Dispatch, 2007.

Mansfield News, *Interview with 105 year-old Miss Reba Williams.* Columbus, Ohio. 2012. Video: https://youtu.be/i2mfbw74HRg

Marshall, Kathy L. *Interviews with Dale Carter.* Columbus, Ohio: Multiple dates. Telephone and video.

Marshall, Kathy L. *Interviews with M. Lavata and Reba Williams.* Columbus, Ohio. Multiple dates. Telephone and video.

Marshall, Kathy L. *Mary Ellen Marshall: The Life of a Hero, Educator, Mother, Artist, Citizen, Mentor and Friend.* Elk Grove, CA. 2015.

Marshall, Kathy L. *Thomas Richard Marshall, A Life Well-Lived, 1931-2014*. Elk Grove, CA. 2014.

Marshall, Mary E. *Reflections From a Mother's Heart: Your Life Story in Your Own Words.* Journal entries were collected from 1998 to 2006: 14, 15, 18, 22, 24, 29, 34, 39, 46, 51, 56, 65, 72, 84, 86, 96, 97, 99, 103, 133, 135, 179, 189. Book created by A. J. Countryman. Dallas: Word Publishing, Inc., 1995.

Miller, Anne. *Celebrating 100 Years with Reba May Williams, Born January 23, 1907*. Columbus, Ohio: Around Town News, Weather, Sports, 2007. DVD from TV News Show.

Poe, Edgar A. *The Tell Tale Heart*. Boston: The Pioneer, 1843.

Whitmire, Lou. *Reba Williams, cook at Malabar Farm, dies at 107.* Mansfield, Ohio: Mansfield News Journal, USA Today Network. 2014.

Wray, Jennifer. *Family, Church Celebrate Centenarian.* Columbus, Ohio: Northland News. 2007.

Yahoo News: Odd News. *106-year-old woman finally gets high school diploma*. 2013.
Video: https://www.youtube.com/watch?v=gGFJyi3SnUo

End Notes

1 *Roots: The Saga of an American Family* is an American television miniseries based on Alex Haley's 1976 novel, *Roots: The Saga of an American Family*. The series first aired on ABC-TV in January 1977.

2 A webinar is a seminar conducted over the internet. Source: www.dictionary.com

3 A Silver Life Master Bridge Player has earned at least 1000 master points. The American Contract Bridge League permits nationwide members to know their approximate overall ranking relative to every other member to reflect the level of competition (e.g., black, silver, ruby, gold). Source: www.acbl.org

4 *Average Annual Wage and Salary Payments in Ohio 1916 to 1932: Bulletin of the United States Bureau of Labor Statistics*, No. 613, page 59.

5 A Mill-rite/millwright is a craftsman or tradesman who installs, dismantles, repairs, reassembles, and moves machinery in factories, power plants, and construction sites. Source: Merriam-Webster Dictionary.

6 Eastern Star: the wife of a Master Mason could become a member of the Order of the Easter Star, which is based on teachings from the Bible. Source: www.EasternStar.org

7 Mason: a brick mason, or bricklayer. Freemason: A member of the brotherhood of Freemasonry, people who have social events for the community that focus on belief in God and brotherhood. www.urbandictionary.com

8 A treadle sewing machine is one that is powered mechanically by a small flat bar foot pedal that is pushed back and forth by the operator's foot. Source: Merriam-Webster Dictionary.

9 Jay Leno hosted some of the biggest celebrities in the world on The Tonight Show with Jay Leno, NBC TV channel, from 1992 to 2014. He mentioned Reba Williams receiving her diploma at 106 in March 2013.

10 The Associated Press delivers in-depth coverage on today's Big Story including top stories, international, politics, lifestyle, business, entertainment, and more. A Google search on "Associated Press Reba Williams 106" found numerous news story results, some even translated into other languages. March 2013.

11 *Same ol' same ol'* was a favorite expression of Reba Williams, especially when asked how she was doing; it meant "everything is the same as it always is."

12 "Guideposts" include newsletters, blogs, Bible verses, and inspiring stories www.guideposts.org

13 Jerry Revish, *Stars' Families Return To Ohio's Hollywood Hideaway.* www.10TV.com. Published 6/27/2012.

14 "Celebrating 100 Years with Reba May Williams Born January 23, 1907" DVD mailed by Lavata Williams to Kathy Marshall who played the video to her dying mother, Mary Marshall, on January 26, 2007.

15 The four-story Woodward Opera House was the oldest opera theater of its kind in the United States, built in 1851, is located in downtown Mount Vernon, Ohio. http://www.thewoodward.org.

16 "Family, Church Celebrate Centenarian," Northland TV News featured Reba William's 100th birthday.

17 Interview with 105 year-old Miss Reba Williams. Columbus, Ohio: 2012. Video: https://youtu.be/i2mfbw74HRg

18 June 26, 2012, Interview with Reba Williams by an unknown source: https://youtu.be/i2mfbw74HRg

19 The **Hare Krishna** movement is a branch of Hinduism. Its name comes from its chant — **Hare Krishna** — which devotees repeat to return to a pure state of consciousness. Source: www.harekrishna.com

20 Dan Vergano: Cruel Medical Experiments On Slaves Were Widespread In The American South, BuzzFeed News, posted April 28, 2015.

21 Rebecca Skloot, "The Immortal Life of Henrietta Lacks," Penguin Random House LLC, 2010.

22 The Congress of Racial Equality (CORE) is an African-American civil rights organization, founded in 1942. CORE's nonviolent direct action campaigns opposed "Jim Crow" segregation and job discrimination, and fought for voting rights. Source: https://en.wikipedia.org/wiki/Congress_of_Racial_Equality

23 Current Mount Vernon, Ohio Population, Demographics and stats in 2016, 2017.
Source: https://suburbanstats.org/population/ohio/how-many-people-live-in-mount-vernon

24 Serials, more specifically known as Movie serials, Film serials or Chapter plays, are short subjects originally shown in theaters in conjunction with a feature film. They were extended motion pictures broken into a number of segments called "chapters" or "episodes". Each chapter was screened at the same theater for one week and ended with a cliffhanger in which the hero and heroine found themselves in a perilous situation with little apparent chance of escape.
Source: http://www.imdb.com/list/ls056855917/

25 A Charlie Brown Christmas is a 1965 animated television special based on the comic strip Peanuts, by Charles M. Schulz.

26 Trimming the windows refers to decorating a window in a shop displaying items for sale or otherwise designed to attract customers to the store. Usually, the term refers to larger windows in the front façade of the shop. The more enticing the display, the more likely customers would enter the store to buy merchandise. https://en.wikipedia.org/wiki/Display_window

27 Apple donates 64K Apple IIe computers to Camellia Basic Elementary School, creating the first Computer lab in Sacramento, while Mary Marshall was the Principal: http://hackeducation.com/2015/02/25/kids-cant-wait-apple.

28 Auntie Mame movie, starring Rosalind Russell, Warner Bros., 1958

29 Columbus Delano, (1809-1896) was a lawyer, rancher, banker, and U.S. Congressman who became a Republican when the party was founded as the major anti-slavery party, advocating federal protection of African-Americans civil rights, and served as President Ulysses S. Grant's Secretary of the Interior. Source:

30 Quints drums: Tenor drums are used as a marching percussion instrument, mounted sets of 4-6 drums allowing one person to carry and play multiple drums simultaneously. https://en.wikipedia.org/wiki/Tenor_drum

31 An Ironman Triathlon is one of a series of long-distance races consisting of a 2.4-mile swim, a 112-mile bicycle ride and a marathon 26.22-mile run, raced in that order and without a break. One of the most difficult one-day sporting events in the world. Source: https://en.wikipedia.org/wiki/Ironman_Triathlon

32 Thurston, Doug, Tom McClelland, Cynci Calvin *Eppie's Great Race: How It All Began*. They reported in 1999 that: "Dr. Thomas Marshall completed his 25th straight race, missing only the inaugural event because he didn't know about it." http://assets.ngin.com/attachments/document/0023/5244/EGR_history.pdf

33 Thomas Marshall preferred to use the term "Afro-Americans" when speaking about black Americans.

34 The Great Migration was the mass movement of five or six million southern blacks to the north and western parts of America between 1915 and 1960. Source: www.blackpast.org.

35 A "shotgun house" is a house n which all the rooms are in direct line with each other usually front to back. Source: Merriam-Webster dictionary.

36 The Tell-Tale Heart, Edgar Allen Poe, 1843. http://www.poemuseum.org/the-tell-tale-heart.

37 Carter E. Sparks was an architect known for designing large custom homes with lots of glass and wood that blended in with the surroundings: http://eichlerific.blogspot.com/2009/11/carter-sparks-architect.html.

38 The Young Men's Christian Association is a nonprofit worldwide organization, founded in 1844, aims to be a leading organization for youth development, healthy living and social responsibility. Source: http://www.ymca.net.

39 Hot pants: very short and usually tight-fitting shorts for women and girls, first popularized in the early 1970s. Source: http://www.dictionary.com/browse/hot-pants.

40 In the 1970's, tall-rubber heeled Famolare shoes aided natural movement. Source: http://www.famolare1969.com.

41 Soul Train was an African-American music-dance television program from 1971 to 2006, featuring R&B, soul, dance/pop and hip hop artists, jazz, and gospel music. Source: https://en.wikipedia.org/wiki/Soul_Train.

42 The Black Panther Party for Self-Defense, was a revolutionary party, to patrol Black neighborhoods to protect residents from police brutality. Source: https://www.britannica.com/topic/Black-Panther-Party.

43 Afrocentrism (also Afrocentricity) is a cultural ideology or worldview that focuses on the history of traditional black African values. Source: https://www.britannica.com/topic/Afrocentrism.

44 Farrah Fawcett hairstyle: This iconic hairstyle, made famous by Charlie's Angels star Farrah Fawcett, was feathered flips cascading down the sides and the back.

45 “Live the Dream” refers to Martin Luther King’s “I Have a Dream Speech” that he delivered at the March on Washington in 1963. Source: https://www.biography.com/people/martin-luther-king-jr-9365086.

46 MacGyver: action-adventure TV series where secret agent Angus MacGyver solves complex problems by making things out of ordinary objects, Source: https://en.wikipedia.org/wiki/MacGyver

CPSIA information can be obtained
at www.ICGtesting.com
Printed in the USA
FSHW020755270119
55290FS